GUIDED MESSAGES
FROM THE **OTHER SIDE**
a spiritual journey

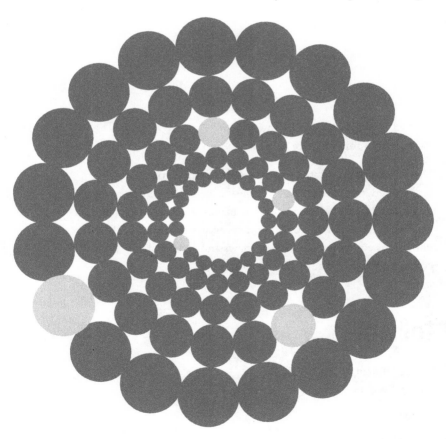

MIKE ELLIS

Tellwell Talent
www.tellwell.ca

ISBN
978-1-77302-272-7 (Hardcover)
978-1-77302-270-3 (Paperback)
978-1-77302-271-0 (eBook)

To Stephanie and Tyler.

You can be all that you want to be. Above all else be happy.

Love Pampa.

There are a number of people I would like to thank. First, my family and friends, for being part of my world, and helping me to be the person I have become. It's been quite a ride, with more to come.

Special thanks to Muzz and Nash, for helping me through some rough patches. Also, thanks to my other family at work, Glenn, Rip, Yossi, Dan and Jeff. Special thanks to Kenny for sharing your books and your thoughts.

And, to the night shift, Jackson, Deo, and Wilbert.

I would like to thank all the messengers who wrote those wonderful books. I loved the ' Abraham ' books and tapes by Jerry and Esther Hicks. The inspiration from Dr. Wayne Dyer, Deepak Chopra, Sylvia Browne, Sonia Choquette, Mike Dooley, Anita Moorjani, and all the ' Conversation with God ' books from Neale Donald Walsch which rang so true to my core. All of these came to me just at the right time. Just when I needed them, the Universe provided.

A special thanks to thank Verine. I wouldn't be who I am without her.

To Stephanie and Tyler, keep dreaming, and always believe, believe, believe. Your dreams will come true. Most of all, be happy. I love you more than you can know.

I am thankful for my teachers and guides for their love, support and inspiration.

Finally, there would be no book, nor would I be even slightly enlightened without Claudette. She has played such an important role in my advancement, and hopefully there will be continued progress as my journey continues.

Blessings to all.

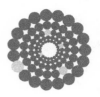

TABLE OF CONTENTS

FROM THE LOWEST...

So, where does one start a story? I've decided to begin at the absolute lowest point in my life. It's November, 2004. I'll be 58 in March.

I must say right at the outset that I'm totally embarrassed and more than a little humiliated to write this, where all who know me or think they do will read this.

But, no matter how stable one may seem, we never really know what that person may be going through, or that even the most stable of us, can have circumstances reach a point that rocks their foundations.

I had finally reached the point where I had had enough. I didn't want to go through with this anymore. I wanted out. *Please,* God let my heart stop beating right now! Let me go. I'm so tired.

The constant worry about how I was going to pay the rent, buy food, pay bills had reached unbearable proportions. I was totally broke. Nothing. This was it. How could I die, and put an end to this.

There must be a way to die that looks natural. It was November, 2004, rainy and cold. I was down at our get-away place in Birch Bay, just over the border in Washington State, less than an hour from Richmond, British Columbia.

If I stand outside in this pouring rain in only a short T shirt and jeans, surely the cold and wet will take the heat from my body, putting stress on my system and maybe heart. After all, I hadn't been eating much, and had lost some weight. At the very least, I can hope for pneumonia. That might kill me if I didn't get any medical attention. What kind of condition could my heart be in anyway? I had abused my body as much, or more so than a lot of people. I loved hamburgers, pizza, French fries, and all of those other fast foods, not to mention doing more than my fair share of drinking in my twenties. Surely, at this age, any real stress could do it.

I stood outside for an hour and a half in the afternoon. Soaked and shivering uncontrollably. Teeth chattering. Body shaking in spasms. This has *got* to do it.

Now, I go into the trailer, without heat, sit in the cold and wait. I sit in the dark for hours, shaking, and praying that my heart will burst. A quick severe pain and it will all be over. When they find me it will look natural, maybe accidental. That's my thinking.

Can you will your heart to stop beating? I try that. Not so far. I sit in the chair, in the dark for hours. I'm still shaking, and very cold. I'm asking the powers that be to take me. I know this is not right, but I have reached 'the end of my tether' as they say. Even if it means I die, and have to come right back and do this over, I still want to go.

Half way through the night, I've more or less dried out, but am still very cold. I go to bed. No blankets. Shaking. Lying there, again trying to make my heart stop. At some point, I fall asleep. I awaken, cold. I'm still here. This hasn't worked. I put myself through all that, and not so much as a sniffle. Good constitution. Thanks, dad, thanks mom.

Well, what about over-stressing the heart. Like I said, I haven't been eating much or well. I, actually, went four days without any food at all. I didn't have enough money. Never did that before. The quick weight loss doesn't look good. Extra skin that needs tightening. Who cares.

Maybe, a good hard run will do it. I put on my sneakers, and start out on my usual walk route. Once I get into the State Park, I begin running, and then running harder, and harder. This will definitely work. I can almost feel my heart ready to explode. It is beating wildly. But then my breath runs out, and I stop. My heart is still really pounding though, and this may just work. I walk on. I do feel dizzy and out of sorts. But no. I try another hard run. Then walk. I make it back to the trailer. Not to be this weekend. Again, thanks mom, thanks dad.

(Now to anyone who has considered ending it all, this may seem like a pathetic attempt. One's thinking isn't always clear when in such a situation. But, there is a stigma attached in my thinking, and I wanted this to seem as though it were occurring naturally. I didn't want my family to go through the pain of my suicide. It wasn't to be, and I now believe it was because there were things that I needed to do. I needed to find out that no matter how badly my life seemed, it wasn't all that bad. That I could come through this, and maybe even find that it could be better than I hoped.)

How did things get to this impasse? How after working for forty years, could I windup at this stage of my life in such a predicament? Well, it started to go bad when Verine, my wife (since separated) was diagnosed with lung cancer. Even worse was when I got a call at work from a doctor, apologizing over and over, finally telling me that the tumor had metastasized*. It was Terminal. With radiation and chemotherapy, they could give her two years, no more.

(* Metastatic cancer is cancer that has spread from the place where it first started, to another place in the body. A tumor formed by metastatic cancer cells is called a metastatic tumor or a metastasis. Metastatic cancer has the same name and the same type of cancer cells as the original, or primary, cancer. Although some types of metastatic cancer can be cured with current treatments, most cannot. -*Taken from the National Cancer Institute Website.*)

This is why the doctor had been so apologetic.

These treatments were grueling. She couldn't continue working. This meant less money coming in. We could still get by though, except other things started to go wrong. I couldn't seem to make any money trading. (I was Head of Trading for a firm in the Brokerage Industry, first on the floor of the Vancouver Stock Exchange, later in the office, after the business went computerized.) No matter what I did, it just wasn't working for me. I was no longer getting a salary. I had to rely on making money in the market.

Credit cards started maxing out. Bills had to be paid, not to mention the mortgage. As many of you know, and probably have experienced to some extent, this seems to roller-coaster out of control. Eventually, we decided to sell our house. We kept our weekend place in Birch Bay.

We moved into an apartment, and put a lot of stuff in storage. This wasn't too bad.

It could have been worse. Well, it got worse for me. I still for the life of me couldn't get anything to go right. (Later on, when I got through all of this, and had done a lot of reading, I understood that this was something I had to go through, to change.) But, at the time, you wonder how can this be happening? Why won't *anything* work?

Meanwhile, Verine had been having a very tough time. She had done twenty radiation treatments, and now was well into the chemo. It got to the point where she couldn't do anymore. She told her oncologist she couldn't finish the treatments. She actually felt like the chemo was going to kill her. I have tremendous admiration for everyone who goes through these treatments, especially when you have a death sentence hanging over your head. And that thought is always with you. It's amazing that they can sleep at all. I can't even imagine the worries, the nightmares that the dark brings.

We would go down to our trailer at Birch Bay on the weekends. Soon, I started coming back as usual on Sunday, for work Monday, while Verine stayed down longer. It's a beautiful spot. Our place is surrounded by wonderful fir trees that are twelve feet high and act as a solid barrier around the perimeter, making it quite private.

There is so much greenery, and it is very peaceful, especially during the week when there's not so many people around. It was a good place for Verine to rest and recuperate.

We had a rather large line-of-credit on the house which we had used to pay for a number of things to do with the trailer and improvements to the house. So, when we sold the house, even though it had appreciated in value over the years, it still took quite a chunk from what we received.

So, here we were, I going down on weekends, and Verine staying there, a good part of the time.

Things weren't getting any better, and I recall one evening during the week, when Verine called on her cell. I was a little down, and I said to her "Maybe you'd be better off without me". The pressure was getting to me. Verine was eight years older than me, though you wouldn't know it to look at her, and could now get her pensions. Her expenses were low, and she could get by better on her own.

She had either been thinking that, or my saying it got her thinking. She had enough worries with her illness, which by this time didn't seem to be getting worse. She sure didn't need added concerns.

It was a couple of months after this, that she told me she thought it would be better if we separated. She told me it was the hardest thing she had ever had to do. Though we had drifted apart somewhat lately, I believe that she was doing it for me. Her illness was hanging over both our heads, and maybe with us separated, I could better serve myself. It was either that, or get off the sinking ship. I choose to believe the former. I wasn't totally surprised, but it was still sad. We had been married for 24 years, and gone out two before that. There had never been arguments or bad scenes. It had been a good marriage, but things change, and I believe that *we* are changing all the time. I certainly was nowhere near the same person that I was when I was younger. It's hard for me to even recognize myself as that person in his late teens and twenties. One's interests change, and unless both of you are changing along the same lines, it's easy to drift apart. My hat's off to all those who make it forty, fifty years and longer. You've done an amazing job of making things work – of give and take.

So, there's a little background on how I got to this point. Verine found a nice little apartment in a senior's complex, with low rent and is now nicely situated. Except for her fibromyalgia, which she developed after her cancer treatments, and some breathing difficulties caused from the scarring on her lungs, also from the radiation treatments, she is doing alright. Against all odds, she managed to beat the cancer. Her oncologist calls her *his miracle patient*. I also believe her time at Birch Bay helped with the peacefulness, relieving some of the stress, and putting her in a better frame of mind. We're good friends and speak all the time.

I stayed in our apartment for a while, but couldn't afford the rent. I had to move out. I put some more belongings in storage, and went down to the trailer for a short stay until I found a smaller, cheaper apartment.

I was getting by, but barely. There is still a lot of worry and concern. That pressure seems to be always with you, in the background. Even to this day, after I've learned so much, any negative feelings seem to be compounded by those 3:00 o'clock in the morning awakenings. The worry is there, and sleep is hard to come by.

Okay, to continue. It's several months later. I'm just scraping by. One afternoon, I turn on the TV, and am flicking through the channels, as men are want to do, when I see on a PBS station a program titled " Dr Wayne Dyer and 'The Power of Intention'". I begin watching it. What he's saying is very interesting, and sounds like something I want to learn more about. The next day at work, I look up his book on the internet, and see there is an excerpt. I read this and feel inspired. I don't know this at the time, or even until quite awhile later, but the Universe is kicking in.

A week later, I'm at the Barnes and Noble bookstore in Bellingham, Washington, which is about a twenty-five minute drive from the trailer, which I'm still able to get to on the odd weekend. I'm just browsing. I can't really afford to buy anything but I've always loved books, and have been a voracious reader all my life, though mostly fiction. There in front of me, almost like I was led there, is "The Power of Intention", and it's on sale. By now this book has been out for quite a while. Even though I can't really afford it, I decide to buy it.

I read the book, and I read it again, and again. This is glorious stuff. I start to practice some of what I'm learning. Affirmations. A lot of "I ams…. (wealthy, feeling good, in a good place, etc.)". It's not so easy at first because of the negativity I've brought to myself. I have to be diligent in catching myself from negative thoughts. I have also started meditating again. This is something I did way back in my early twenties, when I had an interest at that time in the paranormal. I had done some meditating for a couple of years, but then life sort of gets in the way, and I drifted out of it.

Now, things start coming to me. There is so much information on the internet. I can get the internet at work, and I've joined the local library which has some computers that members can use. I'm surfing around one day at work while it's quiet, and I come across a web site on enhancing one's meditating abilities. It's Bill Harris's *Centerpoint*. There's a demo disc you can send away for, which I do, and not long after, I get the disc. This is great. I enjoy this process, and use it every day for months. I use the demo longer than they say, but I can't really afford to take it to the next level. But, again, I get a bit of money, and get their first disc set. (Are the affirmations working? Is the Universe helping me out?) I used this system for a few years.

The fellow I sit next to at work, K., started in the business around the same time that I did. We've both worked for different firms over the years, and now here we are, and there is a relevance to this, and again how things work. I happened to mention to K. that I'd found this interesting book "The Power of Intention ". K. says he has already read it. We discuss this a bit, and I learn that K. is extremely interested in these sorts of books, and he'll bring me in a book he thinks I'll like. It's one of Sylvia Browne's books. I don't remember which one. Verine and I had actually read a couple of her early books. So, K. and I talk some more, and I learn he has quite a library of spiritual books. He lends me more of Sylvia Browne's works.*

*(Sylvia Browne had written a number of books on Angels, Spirit Guides, many aspects of the Other Side, being Psychic, and a great deal more.)

So, by this time, I'm surfing different web sites, and subscribing to some, and I'm receiving daily inspirational emails sent to me from certain sites, when one day, I get an email about a new book out by Neale Donald Walsch called " A Conversation with God."

Conversations with God? What's that all about? I go to the web page and read a bit of the history behind this creation. This sounds way out there. Is this for real? Once again, I'm down south, and I go to Barnes & Noble. They have a couple of the *CWG* books. I buy Book I. I read it. **WHAM.** It is awesome. I am overwhelmed. Emotional.

This is incredible. This book rings so true to me. I feel it inside. It makes sense, even though I have trouble getting my head around some of it. NOBODY could make this up. I read it again.

I tell K. what I've found. Well wouldn't you know it, he's got *all* the books. He lends me Book II, and then Book III, and over time, one by one all the rest.

So, are you wondering if something is guiding me along here? I don't believe in coincidences any more. Something is definitely happening, almost on cue. Books come into my hands just at the right moment, almost in order of relevance to what I need at that time. Or an email will come to my inbox with just the right '*thought for the day*' that I needed to hear. Mind you I'm starting to be more aware of this sort of thing, more so than I would have been in the past, when I wouldn't have thought twice about it.

(Now might be a good time to comment on where I am at this point. So, going back to the beginning of this book, my heart did not explode the way I hoped it would. It wasn't meant to. I had other things to do. I managed to crawl through all of that with the help of the UNIVERSE/GOD/SOURCE, and get to where I am now - hopefully, a better person, who is looking forward to a new age, where we are more enlightened, more conscious of who we really are.)

The next progression is about to unfold.

CLAUDETTE

Just prior to this Verine had suffered a devastating loss. Verine had two children from a previous marriage, a boy C. and a girl Lisa. C. had moved out by the time we married and Lisa about a year later. Both kids accepted me, which is not always the case, and we got along great.

So, around the time that Verine and I had been apart for a few months, Lisa was diagnosed with lung cancer, just like her mom. She was a smoker, and a wonderful loving person. This happened just as things started really going well for her. She'd just bought her first home, she had the car of her dreams, a good job, and everything couldn't be going better...then this.

I will always maintain that Verine was spared her death sentence so that she could be there for Lisa. No one could know better what she was going through. Verine moved in with Lisa and helped her through all the treatments, made sure she got to her appointments, picked up her medicines, along with the regular household chores. She also got Lisa to try the Center for Integrated Healing, which Verine did, and to this day believes it helped her beat the cancer. (Along with her regular cancer treatments, Verine went to the Center for Integrated Health, taking mega vitamins. She also practiced *Visualization* techniques; every day visualizing the tumor shrinking.)

Unfortunately for Lisa, it wasn't to be. She got worse. She was having trouble breathing, and her lung capacity was severely reduced. She had to obtain oxygen tanks to assist her. Eventually, she had to go to the hospital, and again Verine was there most of the time, except for the odd break, which she needed herself, for she still wasn't completely well, and to this day has shortness of breath. Lisa was hardly ever alone though, there were always friends to stay with her, but no one was there more, or more appreciated than her mother.

The next move was to palliative care, which is the hardest move of all, because there's only one way out, and that's when reality strikes, and there are scary, and heart-wrenching moments. Verine was with Lisa pretty much constantly, and slept in the room on a small bed. The two of them could not be any closer then, through these remaining days. I visited when I could, but many times I was set to go, and Verine said Lisa just wasn't well enough for a visit. It can be draining with too many people around, when you're not feeling well. But, we shared some good moments with talks of happier times.

She was a trooper right to the end.

I got the call from Verine on May 1st that Lisa had passed that morning. Verine said she had a small smile on her face.

This was very hard on Verine. Verine had raised both kids by herself from the time they were very young. The two had become even closer, if that's possible, in the past few months. As they say, "You're not supposed to outlive your kids".

Verine was very strong through the funeral, but it was afterwards, when she was on her own, that she was having trouble dealing with this terrible loss. And, as time went by, it wasn't getting any better. Eventually, her doctor recommended professional help. She had several sessions with a psychologist, and in one session he got around to her religious beliefs.

We had both been raised as Roman Catholics. I got away from all organized religions when I left home. There just seemed like too much hypocrisy for me. Verine was disillusioned with the church after it basically excommunicated her after her divorce, even though it wasn't her fault.

Anyway, her doctor asked if she believed in life after death, which she did. He suggested she see this medium he knew about in Steveston, an area in the southwest of Richmond, a suburb of Vancouver. Verine called me with this information, and asked what I thought about her going, she knew I was a lot more into this kind of thing than she was. The first thing both of us thought was 'Wow'; this isn't something you usually hear from someone in the medical profession. I thought that was very cool. I was all for this. I mean it couldn't hurt trying it. In truth, this may have been a little more desirous on my part, for this was definitely an area I had always been interested in, but how do you find a medium, when there are so many charlatans out there. What could be better than finding one recommended by a professional person?

Verine made her appointment. Went. And I won't go into details of her session, but it went well, and I believe it helped to start her healing process. Now, Verine wouldn't tell anyone else about this, because there are a lot of skeptics, and non-believers out there, and I can respect that. But, she knew I was very excited to hear what happened. Everyone is given a tape of their session, and she gave me hers to listen to. I listened to the tape, and immediately knew this was something I had to do. (What happened in her session belongs to her).

At this time, I was squeaking by financially. I was able to pay the minimum on my bills. I had started to apply some of what I had been reading in the different books. I was using a lot of affirmations, and trying to change my thinking. It's not an easy turn around. You don't realize how many thoughts are constantly going through your head. One's mind is never still, even while meditating it takes a lot of concentration to calm those thoughts. Like everything, it gets easier the more you practice. It's really hard to monitor your thoughts all day long. Later, I would learn there is a better way, by focusing on your emotions. The amount of negative and worrisome thoughts is overwhelming, and it's all because of what took place years earlier, as far back as our childhood. Like constantly hearing, "Money doesn't grow on trees", or "Money is the root of all evil", "We're not made of money" etc. Now, I wouldn't say our family was considered poor. My mother had to work, when most mothers at that time stayed home. And, I know my parents went without a lot, so that we were fed and clothed. There was always food on the table though, and gifts under the tree at Christmas. My mother was a fantastic cook, but if she was going to be late, my Dad, who worked nights, was not bad at getting the evening meal ready.

So, anyway, all these sayings we were brought up with, become deeply ingrained in our psyche, and you just don't change decades of beliefs overnight. I found myself constantly repeating lines like "Money is good, I like money", "I attract money", "Money flows to me", "I am a money magnet", and then believing, believing, believing.

Okay, I was getting by at least.

Now, back to Claudette.

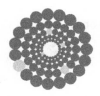

FIRST SESSION

It was a few months later, when I had a few extra bucks, that I decided to phone and make an appointment with the medium. The lady's name was Claudette, and she told me to think of some questions, and to concentrate for a couple of days prior, on who I wanted to come through to me.

Claudette has a centre called, "The Wings of Doves". The following are excerpts taken from her brochure: "Doves have always been associated with peace, love and the feminine aspect of healing energies. ' Wings of Dove 'are the carrier wings that transport energy vibrations of Love and Light".

Claudette is an International medium who left the corporate environment over 20 years ago. She began her traveling journey of healing, studying and working with spiritual energies that took her to England, the U.S. and across Canada.

She conducts a number of Therapies, including Reiki – a natural method of healing for adults, children, animals, and even plants; Energy medicine; Animal Energy Healing; Fundamentals of Restructuring Emotional/Mental Energy Obstructions; Past Life Regression, (another session I can't wait to try); Clearing of Negative Energies; and Channelling & Mediumship.

She also has a number of workshops such as: Finding Your Souls' Voice/Sound; Creative Art with Spirit and Angels; Message Life – from loved ones in afterlife; Trance Channelling; Yoga Meditation, and more.

It's now April 12, 2006 and my appointment was at 2:00 pm. I was very excited. I entered her place, which was situated on a tidy side street, along with several other small shops. You walk directly into the room where the session takes place. It was nicely decorated, with a desk with chairs on either side. There was another room in the back separated by curtains.

Shortly after I entered, Claudette came through to greet me. She asked me to have a seat and made me feel welcome right away. She had a slight accent (French?). She was smiling, and there was a very friendly demeanor about her. She said this was a little different for her, having a male coming in for a reading. Obviously, most of her customers were female, which I could understand. Somehow, men seem more skeptical, or at the very least much less likely to go this far, and they certainly wouldn't admit it if they did. Even I haven't told anyone that I was doing this, other than Verine, and K. who I knew would be interested.

She checked that there was a tape in the recorder between us, and began by asking me to relax and breathe deeply. She then said a prayer, and said that spirit was present.

Now, might be a good time to mention that the spirit world, and the spirits themselves, are on a totally different vibrational wavelength than us - a much higher frequency. So, it's not always straightforward as to who is coming through, and it is not always easy for the medium to pick up who it is that is trying to make themselves understood. Claudette gets feelings, words, pictures, and the pictures oftentimes have to be deciphered by the person getting the reading. The first one to come through was a female presence with a motherly complex. Claudette asked if my mother was in spirit, which she wasn't. Then asked about my grandmother, who was. I only knew one grandparent growing up, and that was my grandmother on my mother's side. She lived with us until I was six, and then returned to England.

It was her coming through, Claudette said, with tremendous love, and saying she was sorry that she couldn't have been around longer for me.

There was also a male present, who she thought might be my grandfather, who I hadn't known, but my mother had told me about. She said he had big hands, was a big man, and that I was very much like him.

I immediately thought of my father, who had passed twelve years before. He was 6'3" and had huge mitts, and I did resemble him, only a smaller version.

I mentioned this, and she agreed now that this was who was coming through. She asked me if we had clashed prior to his passing. I said no, everything had been fine between us. She said my father was saying that he felt bad, and wanted to apologize, and that he hadn't understood at the time, and that he does understand now that he's here. She asked if my father had been strict. (Yes, he had been very strict, and heaven help you if you got out of line when you were a kid, and I did. I had been a bit of a rebel, and often paid the price. When he said you'd get a thick ear, he meant it. It was a different time then – spare the rod, spoil the child. You wouldn't get away with that now. But it only happened if you did something wrong, and you knew ahead of time that it was a consequence. He was also, probably the most stubborn man I ever knew, but he loved us all, and as we got older, even though we didn't see each other much, he had moved to Vancouver Island, we were still close. There was nothing he loved better, once we were older, than going to the pub for a few games of darts, and some drinks.)

So, I said out loud, "Dad there's nothing to forgive, but I do forgive you, if you need to hear the words".

Claudette: "He also says he's very proud of you – proud of the distance that you've come." She says she has the feeling that it has been a struggle for me, but that she sees me surfacing.

Mike: "I hope I'm still surfacing."

Claudette: "Like you've been underwater, and you come up gasping. Emotional stuff."

Mike: "I understand."

Claudette asks if my father had lung problems – she has the feeling of difficulty of breathing. He had been a heavy smoker, though he quit, maybe 10 years before his death.

Claudette: "Also, he says that there have been some financial difficulties with you."

I agree.

Claudette: "He says he's looking at a ledger, and he says, 'You know, son, we're going to have to do something about this.'"

She then asked if I had my own business. I reply "No". She asks if Dad had his own business. Again, "No". She says she is seeing me with my own business and she feels that Dad is going to help me bring this ledger to a greater benefit to me. Dad says it's time for me to get out of this rut.

Mike: "I appreciate it".

Claudette says she 'sees this rut as having my feet stuck in mud, and my Father is giving me a hand getting out of this mud. "Father is going to help you locate something that is more lucrative for you". She asks if I'm bored with work. I tell her I've done it a long time, and it can get boring when it's slow, and we are coming on to the summer months when the market, generally slows down. (I love the guys I work with though. They're like family). She says I'm ready for a change. She's seeing a career change. She sees my father helping me make a change or shift in environment.

Claudette: "Who would have worked for the railroad, or near a railroad?" She's seeing a railroad like the pioneering days. She asks if I have an uncle who has passed. I have a few that have passed, but again, only one I really knew. My uncle George on my mother's side, who I liked very much, passed when I was around 17, of cancer, but he worked in the Aero industry. This isn't him.

She says she's seeing a railroad in the mountains, and then asks "Who would have gone gold mining? An adventure." She is seeing an uncle figure. (This wasn't registering with me.) She says "I'm seeing someone who is going on an adventure saying "Yeah, lets try it". (This still isn't making any sense to me.) She explains that this person had a good sense of humor, and was light weight (not physically), didn't take himself too seriously. Made light of things, though felt very deeply. (I just couldn't place anyone to this.)

(Now I want to come back to this later, because this goes along with what I was saying earlier, about the sending of pictures, to get across who is trying to come through.)

We leave this and Claudette states "You are very sensitive. There's a deep sense in you, a feeling in sensing things. Do you understand? And for a part of your life you looked at this as a curse. It's not a curse, it's an asset. There were times when you took on someone else's emotional crap, and lived it. You need to protect yourself with the *Golden Spear of Energy*." (I'll have to find out more about this.)

She further says "You are psychic, intuitive in many things, and anytime you don't listen to your abilities or intuition, you pay for it."

I reply that I have actually been working on developing some of what she has been saying, through my meditations.

Claudette: "You need to develop that because it is a part of who you are".

She then asks if I have Scottish in my family. I say that as far as I know, most of my family is from England, with maybe a little Belgium thrown in. She says "Okay, I'm getting the U.K. here. I'm really seeing the Island, England, and Ireland. I want to say that as I touch your energy, I see that spark come on, and that would indicate that you have sensitivity to spirit. To your ability to do…to do what I'm doing, and that you really need to develop that, and as I say that I see a gentleman standing on your left side, and I feel that he would be a guide, and I get the name Arthur. His name is Arthur. 'Sir Arthur'. I don't believe it is King Arthur, but I feel that he would have had position, status – lord of the land, wherever that was."

(I had mentioned earlier that when making the appointment with Claudette, she asked me to focus for a couple of days ahead of time, on those I wanted to come through. I was really interested and hoping that one of those would be a spirit guide).

Claudette: "*Thank you**. I want to say east, southeast. 'Do you understand, please?' We're going towards *the Seven Sisters*. (Later, I had to look this up. It's down towards Dover on the south coast of England). Okay. (Claudette chuckles). I'm getting some history on England now. I want to say that you've come from very ancient land, layers and layers of history. 'Do you understand'? I feel that it's not by chance that you were born there. You were born within some very sacred land. 'Do you understand'? I feel that at this time in your life, that it's time you developed your abilities to do your spiritual work as well, but it doesn't mean letting go of one to do the other, it means blending and merging the both of them and that your guides…..'Do you believe in Angels, please'? ('Yes.')

* (This is Claudette getting info from her Spirit Guide.)

Claudette: "*Yes, thank you.* I'm seeing some angels around you; particularly Archangel Michael is with you. It's like you've had to stand up for yourself, and defend yourself. 'Do you understand, please'? And, I feel that you've come out of some very bad situations recently. ('Oh yeah'). 'How the hell, oops, how did I get out of that?' Do you understand, please?"

Mike: "Yes".

Claudette: "I want to say that this is the work of the Archangel Michael, helping you and so on, because you really do have work to be done in your spiritual abilities. When you have the gift, it's your responsibility to use it to the betterment of mankind, right?"

('Yes.')

Claudette: "And so I feel that the call is being made because now I'm seeing Gabriel with the trumpet, 'wake up, it's time'. May I ask how old you are?"

('59.')

Claudette: "59. See you're going to be hitting 60 and there again is that six year time progress, right?" And so, when is your birthday."?

('March 27th..')

Claudette: "Okay, so you just turned 59. So, you're working on your 60th year, and '*yes, thank you*', you are in that process of shifting and changing, making that change, and I want to say at this time in your life, it's time for you. Do you understand? Where you're going to bring in that spirituality. And you had your work with the material world...it doesn't mean you're going to give up your material ... .no, no, no. It means you're going to bring in your spiritual, or allow your spirit to grow, so that you can be more productive, more lucrative. Do you understand, please"?

Mike; "I've been working on that, actually, for the last little while, Trying to..."

Claudette: "To get it together".

('Yes'.)

Claudette: "It's in the works, because when I looked at you, I saw that blue and green, indigo, etc. and indigo to me is the Buddha colour, and the other blue was your throat chakra. So, I feel that spirit wants to work through your throat chakra, so that would indicate clairaudience, which means hearing spirit. Do you understand? Have you heard spirit? Yes, you did as a child particularly, you heard spirit. I want to go back to when you were just a young boy, you would have been anywhere from 8 to 12. I get 11 and 12 years old. It's like you heard your name or you heard something."

Mike: "You know what? I did hear something. But, this would be when I was in my mid twenties, and I had actually tried to meditate and... um... anyway I tried to do certain things, and this particular day, I had a feeling in my stomach that I could come out of my body, and I heard a voice say 'I'm here Michael' and it scared me so much (Claudette chuckles) that I came right out of it, and I thought 'God, that was something'. (Chuckles again). But, it was clear as a bell, if I could do it now, I would actually love to have that happen to me again."

(As I said earlier in this writing, when I was in my early twenties, I was very interested in the paranormal. I had done a bit of reading like *There is a River,* the life story of Edgar Cayce, and some way out books by *Lobsang Rampa,* who was a Tibetan Lama who went to school, I believe in England, and wrote some books on *Astral Travel,*{If I remember the one I read was called *The Third Eye*} and many more interesting topics, some really far out.)

Anyway at that time I was meditating, and trying to have this out of body experience. I thought what a wild experience that would be. But, nothing ever happened, and as I stated, I got away from all of that. So, this is a few years later, and the market got really slow, and I do mean really slow, and I had left the business to go back to school. (A lot of guys in the business at that time left to do other things). I was 29 and attending B.C.I.T. at the time, and working some nights, and summers at the Billy Bishop Legion as a bartender. After working one Thursday night, I got home, and I didn't usually go to bed right away, I was watching television, but feeling very wiped out, and decided to go to bed. I was dead tired but couldn't get to sleep. I had a very fitful night, just sort of dozing, then awakening, and dozing again. This went on until the sun came up. I don't remember ever feeling this tired. It was then that I got this sensation of a whirlwind or vortex around my navel, and my eyes are shut, and I'm not sure if I'm dreaming or what, but I know without a doubt, that at this moment I can come out of my body. I feel myself pulling out, when I hear "I'm here Michael" (in my head) and it is so clear, like someone is standing right next to me with a beautiful voice. However, I got nervous, because in some of those books I read, there was the possibility of entities taking over your body from the astral plane, and though I didn't think that would happen, it was enough to scare me, and I forced myself awake. I got up. I was still really tired, but I wouldn't be sleeping for awhile. So, all those times I had tried for this, and then when I get the opportunity, I blow it. I would love to have that opportunity again. I've learned so very much more since that time about protecting yourself, and feel that this time I would do it. But, who knows if I'll get another chance. I look for that feeling around my navel often. I will never forget that wonderful voice though. Anyway, I have heard spirit.)

Claudette: "See Archangel Michael with Michael, it didn't twing to me. Yes. I heard that you heard spirit, and I also want to say that you heard it as a child, but that you didn't make it any big deal. 'Oh yeah', it's just natural and then it kind of disappeared, and you didn't pay any attention, and so it was a natural thing. It was "so what". It's just the way you took things in those days. Then you got involved and racked up with life, and it got put aside. Do you understand? And so, you tried to cope with life on your own. And now you've come to wisdom that 'hey now I've got to do them both.'"

"And so you do have the gift, and yes the guides are there to work with you, and they do want you to work with it, and often you will hear things in your head, please. You know, like enough to make you think 'am I going nuts'? So, you need to write these down; there's inspirational information coming in, and I also feel that it is your spirit guides that have been trying to wake you up".

"Did your wife have a miscarriage, please? I have a child here. Did you have two wives?"

(This next bit got quite emotional for me, and was the very last thing in the world I could have anticipated happening).

Mike: "No, just the one. I don't think she had a miscarriage. Um. (Then I got a thought of something from years ago). I had a girlfriend... welllll... it wasn't a miscarriage". (Hesitation)

Claudette: "Abortion"?

Mike: "I had a girlfriend who had an abortion".

(This happened around 1972. I was 25, and had been going out with this girl for a while. I got her pregnant, and it was a very big decision for both of us on what to do, but ultimately I thought it was up to her, after all she was the one who had to go through with it. I, also, have to say that this was the seventies. You know that saying that if you can remember the sixties, then you didn't *live* them. Well, I had a couple of years in my twenties that were a little hazy. I can definitely understand her final decision. It's a big responsibility and she probably, and rightfully so, decided that now wasn't the best time. She had the abortion in a hospital. We eventually moved in together, but it only lasted maybe another year. I came home from the bar one day, and she had moved out. I will say that it was mostly my fault, but irregardless, I missed her very much, and I honestly did love her. Anyway, she made the right decision and maybe one day I'll get the opportunity to apologize to her for my lack of attention, and my carousing ways.)

Claudette: "*Thank you.* (To the spirit) That would be it then, miscarriage or abortion, and so it's a child who never drew breath. Right? So I have ......and I want to say it's a boy... ......"

Mike: "Oh, really".

Claudette: "… ….coming forward to say hello to you, because he says 'this is my father'. (My eyes are starting to well up) That's why I wanted to say… … So he's saying 'I'm here'. So he's saying to you it was all meant to be this way. He wasn't meant to live in this world, and he chose the parents because he knew that he would be aborted. Do you understand? It was all meant to be that way. He says don't feel bad, and he doesn't want his mother to feel bad about it. It was all meant to be. But, he says I want you to know that I exist. Do you understand, please?"

Mike: "I'll look forward to seeing him."

Claudette: "Well, he's here but he would also….see the children that have been forgotten, if you like, want to have a name. So, I want you to have a meditation, and give him a name. He's coming as a young boy so that he can be your 'Joy Guide'. Just know…..so that he can cheer you up. So, when you do your next meditation, he'll be there by your side, and just get a sign going between the two of you as to give you some education, that it is him and not your guide or somebody else, you know. So, he says 'I'm here to bring you joy'.

(At my very next meditation I gave him a name…..John Michael Ellis. Everyone in my family has very common names, Michael, Peter, Mark, Susan, my cousins Anne, Dave, Jeff, Kathy, and my father and brother's middle name was John. It came to me pretty quickly, and I was proud to let him have my name. I talk to John all the time, and look forward to the time when we meet.)

Claudette: "And did you sing, please? You sing. You've got a voice."

Mike: "Yes. I always sang."

Claudette: "He's telling me 'he sings'." (Laughing, laughing).

Mike: "I used to sing in the bathroom when I was a kid, all the time. It used to drive my parents crazy."

Claudette: "And he happens to love your voice. He says you need to sing more. Do you understand, please? Even if you have to take singing lessons, you need to sing more, and just sing. But I feel…. my heart's just expanding with him. He's so excited that he's been able to introduce himself. So… just know that…and you bring him peace by being here today, because he's been trying get your attention. Have you had things fall off the counter… or whatever? Or your tool desk?

Mike: "Yes, I have actually. Yes….."

Claudette: "And that's been him trying to get…."

Mike: "…something happened the other day, and I wondered 'how did that fall?'"

Claudette: "There it is. He's been trying to get your attention, right? And, because you're not clicking in yet ….(Chuckle) … you're not listening. So, he's been moving things, or things falling. Do you have a tool room… a tool desk?"

Mike: "A workbench?"

Claudette: *"Yes, thank you."*

Mike: "I have a shed with a lot of tools."

Claudette: "Yes, and wasn't there something that fell not too long ago?"

Mike: 'Yes." (Hammer fell. I couldn't figure out why at the time).

Claudette: "And I want to say that he was responsible for that as well. I'm seeing the typical male tool room. You need a bigger room he says" (Laughing).

Mike: "That's true."

Claudette: "But he also says, there's a lot of you in him. Do you understand, please? So, I feel that he is going to inspire you to be more fluffy… sing or hum, whistle. I hear you whistling. You don't yodel, do you?"

Mike: "No."

Claudette: (Laughing) "I am hearing yodelling. Who in your relatives would yodel?…and I want to say grandparent or great-grandparent."

Mike: "I didn't know them."

Claudette: "I want to say a great-grandparent because I have somebody on the rolling hills. It's got to be somebody from England, the U.K., who would have loved walking, and he went walking and whistling, and he had a walking stick. Very British. Just walking the trail, whistling at the same time, and he says 'you should do a little of that. And I get the letter *S*., Sam, Sanderson … the letter *S*.; I'm not good with names, but the first letter….'"

Mike: "I'll have to ask my mother. I don't really know a lot of them."

Claudette: "Yes, please do. Now, Mom has to look after herself, I understand here from father. She needs to want to start living again. Is she in depression, or not feeling well?"

Mike: "She's eighty-nine, and she's very tired, and she's at the point where she'd just as soon go…"

Claudette: "Right.Yep.Yep.Yep. She's at that 'What am I doing here? No purpose. No reason to be here. This is way too old. I shouldn't have lived this long.' So, we want to say that she is alert…."

Mike: "Yes. Definitely."

Claudette: "…very alert, but she doesn't like herself anymore. So, she's into this 'poor me being old'. So, I feel that you can bring a little life into her, I hear, because she has a soft spot…"

Mike: "I'll tell her that dad said that.

Claudette: "Yeah, because he's really concerned. He is saying,' Come on woman. Get on with it. Just move'. So, I feel another 5 years with her".

Mike: "Really?"

Claudette: "So, I feel that she needs to make it quality time".

Mike: "Absolutely".

Claudette: "But I feel that once she feels that … and again, tell her that your father has been with her. I feel that she misses him".

Mike: "She does, very much. She tells me all the time".

Claudette: "Yes. I want to go back with him. I want to be with him. (' Yes '). I'm lonely here. Everybody has their life, there's nothing left for me. And so, they had their strong relationship. So, she misses him, and you need to tell her that he is with her, and she needs to start feeling him, sensing him, and she needs to start listening to those 'Nonsense' he used to tell her".

"Also, I feel that she wakes up at certain times during the night and she's feeling him around. And so, she would say 'Yeah, I felt him.' (I mentioned this to her on my next visit and she agreed she did feel his presence at times). Because I really feel that she is very psychic, your mom. Very psychic. She knows more about you than you think she knows…"

Mike: "Really?"

Claudette: …"Do you understand? You can't really hide much from her…"

Mike: "No, no. I can see that."

Claudette: …"If she's really wanting to know or paying attention, she can tell, because she's very psychic. She'll be thinking about you and the next thing you know, you'll be calling her. It's that psychic connection between the two of you."

"Any questions before we run out of time?"

Mike: "Um, I guess one of my concerns was how am I doing spiritually, but you've kind of addressed that."

Claudette: "Well, I feel that you need to do more work, and also that you should journal. Journal the things that you hear in your head. Do you understand, please? Don't look at what you're writing, just write. Just write. And, don't try to make sense about what you are writing, okay? Just get yourself a little booklet at the dollar store, and just write whatever is going on in your head. Don't try to make sense, or watch the grammar or anything, because inspirational writing does not lead to quick understanding."

Mike: "I guess, maybe, what a lot of people are interested in is 'how long have I got,' or do they say things like that?"

Claudette: "Oh my God. (Chuckling) You're already concerned about leaving?"

Mike: "No, but I…"

Claudette: "No, you're here for a while yet. Because, you've done what you've had to do, and learned your lessons in the material world, and physical world, and so now you're about to begin really getting into your spiritual merging with your material, and that is a process, right? And I feel that once you commit to that, there's an acceleration to it. Boom, boom, boom, here it is. And I feel excited about that. Okay, I'm ready. No matter what happens in my life, I'm going to dedicate myself to my development. Bang, everything starts happening."

Mike: "I was hoping my wife's daughter might come through, just to see if there was anything I could do for her. But, is there anything I can do for any of them, while I'm here?"

Claudette: "In the spirit world, the best thing is prayer. Healing prayer. *Yes, thank you.*

And I just heard 'I am fine', and I got a shiver through my body. I thought are you the step daughter and I heard 'I am fine. Thank you and I heard your prayers.' You've been talking to her. ('Yes') 'And I have heard you.' *Yes, thank you.* She's making me very cold. (Chuckle) 'Thank you for your generosity and thank you for the love that you have given me, and I truly appreciate that. I'm on the mend.'

("Do you understand?") 'I'm on the mend, and I'm progressing very well. Now, you get on with it.' (Laugh).

"But she was very close, and I feel sadness in her heart, a sadness that she left so quickly. ('Yes'). But we all have our time limits. She says, 'I went and peeked in your book, your file, (in other words your chart), and she says 'you're there, you're going to be doing some great stuff.' She can't say what was there, and she would only be privy to a certain amount of information anyways. (According to some, we have charted out what will take place when we take on our physical existence. These are all kept in the *Hall of Records*.)

"But you're about to begin your true mission, you see? And so, your personal life will develop accordingly. Once you commit to it, then you manifest your personal life to embrace that as well. But, you have a lot of support from your wife, friends and relatives. This is not foreign to your family, you see, whether they want to admit it or not."

"Your family from the other side are coming to support you. You've got an uncle with a great sense of humour… (Laughing) and who would have played the violin or banjo, or something? Uh, I've got a …"

Mike: "A ukulele?"

Claudette: …"Yes. I'm seeing a banjo, instrument…"

Mike: "You know what? My father-in-law played a ukulele."

(Okay, now near the beginning of this session, I said I would come back to the part about the railroad and the rolling hills, and I also mentioned how those on the other side sometimes send pictures. Well, those pictures weren't registering with me. So, it turns out it was my father-in-law, who passed maybe fifteen years ago, who was sending those pictures, and who was now trying to come through with a different picture, one I would recollect when I heard it. My in-laws were great people. They had built a summer place on Heffley Creek Lake, just north of Kamloops in southern central B.C. Kamloops has rolling hills, and there are train tracks going through Heffley Creek. It didn't click with me at the time. A friend of his had a place there two doors over, and loved trying new things. Adventure? One day he got J.D. (my father-in-law) to go gold panning with him at the stream down the road. That hadn't clicked with me either at the time. A father-in-law is like an uncle figure, who Claudette had pictured.)

Claudette: "Alright, *Thank you.* Because ….*thank you*, as you said father-in-law… I'm seeing the instrument, right? And so, he's coming to say hello."

Mike: "Oh yeah, I was hoping they might."

Claudette: "Yes, and he hits you on the back and says, 'What a go, guy'. (Laughing). So he's proud about something you've just done recently. There's something you did out of your heart, and he thanks you for that. There's something to do with his family. Is it his daughter that you're married to? And I feel that there's some support that you've given your wife that he's proud of. Something to do with his daughter, and he's lifting his cup. Did he enjoy a pint or two? (Laughing) (Yes, he liked a rum and coke once in a while) Okay, so he's lifting a glass. (Still laughing)."

"Also, who would have been in the army, the forces during World War II, please? I have somebody coming through in a soldier type uniform."

Mike: "Gee. Most of my relatives were. My dad, uncles ….I had friends that were."

Claudette: "Okay, somebody that died in the war or close after, please? And, I've got a brown uniform. ('Army') Army. Brown uniform."

Mike: "I wonder…"

Claudette: "I feel it would have been British."

Mike: "I wonder if my grandfather….he would…"

Claudette: "Was he a shorter man?"

('Yes, he was'.)

"Because this was a short man, not tall like you. Maybe 5'8". Yes, he's showing me 5'8". Wasn't he the one talking a few minutes ago? He didn't die in the war?" ('No.' And he wasn't in the Second World War. He was in The First and the Boer War. He died around the time of the Second.)

"Oh, that would explain why I got confused. And, I feel that it is him. But, he has the uniform where from the knee down it was really tight. ('Yes. I've seen pictures of him in his uniform.') More room above the knee. Cool. Any other questions, please?"

Mike: "No. Just sort of a lighter question. I was wondering about my dog that passed a while ago. Is that something I can ask?"

Claudette: "I'm seeing a long haired dog. Black & white. What colour was your dog?"

Mike: "Ah well, I did have a black & white lab cross, but the last one was a gray colour."

Claudette: "Was he… the lab… was he long haired? ('Yes') Because when you said dog, I immediately saw this black & white dog, right? And he went *howl*. (Laughing) That's funny. And the other one was also a big dog?"

Mike: 'No. He was a small one. The black & white was bigger. Toby was just a little … he was a Maltese cross… smaller… a house dog."

Claudette: "No. I don't see him. But, I see the bigger dog. Immediately, that dog was right there beside you, sitting on his butt, looking at you. 'What about me?' (Laughing) Were you young when he… ('Yes I was around fourteen.')…So, he's there. I mean that dog was your psychiatrist. You said everything to that dog. Your thoughts, whatever. He was your companion. Yes, when you were younger, because I feel that I get the impression, 'no one understands me' and this dog just got you out of it, so that's why I say he was like your psychiatrist… and so… (Chuckle) now that you've called Toby, he's on your lap." (Laughing)

Mike: "Oh is that right. I really miss him."

Claudette: "You called him. And the two of them have met. They play together. ('Oh, that's good'). When Toby crossed over… what was the name of the first dog? ('Buster'). Buster knew that Toby was coming, and took it upon himself to greet him and say…'I used to be'… And now they're really running in the fields together and doing doggy stuff. So our time is up."

Mike: "Yes, that's great. Thank you very much."

Claudette: "Thank you again."

So, that was my session with Claudette. I was very excited when I left, and couldn't wait to get home and listen to the recording. Those who I had hoped to connect with, had come through, and that absolutely startling discovery that I had a son on the other side that I hadn't even known about, had got me quite emotional.

I was very impressed with the reading.

I've already discussed that part about the railroad and the gold mining, which she saw as an uncle figure but was really my father-in-law. Close enough. She also described him very well. He did make light of things, but also felt very deeply.

There's no doubt that that was my father. Even though I couldn't hear him, it sounded like him, the way he would speak. He talked about me getting out of a rut, and that's exactly what I felt I was in, and he would look for something for me.*

*(I left the brokerage business in March 2008 after forty plus years. In November 2008 I began working for a Security firm as a Security Officer at University of British Columbia Hospital. I worked nights, again with a good bunch of guys, though a lot younger than me, but I held my own.)

The part about me being psychic and intuitive was very interesting. It's definitely something that I have to start working on. I would like to develop that part of me. When I get better situated money wise, I will look into taking one of Claudette's workshops.

As I said earlier, I was glad my spirit guide 'Arthur' came through. It's nice to have a name I can use when I'm looking for guidance. I believe that we have a number of *spirit guides* who have different functions. In Sonia Choquette's book

"Ask Your Guide" she mentions Runner, Helper, Healer, Teacher, Animal, Joy and Light Guides.

Claudette was right when she said I had *heard spirit*. That morning when I heard "I am here, Michael" has stayed with me, and I wish more than anything I had taken it further at the time. I hope I get another chance. I don't recollect hearing anything as a child, but I know that many children are very perceptive with psychic abilities and think nothing of it. Unfortunately, most grow out of it.

I do believe in Angels, and I am sure they have helped me in some difficult, even dangerous situations when I was young and foolish.

Nothing could have prepared me for the part where the child (John) who hadn't drawn breath came through. It was an emotional moment at the time and for a few times after that. He is always in my prayers, and I talk to him often. I feel close to him now, and I'm happy knowing he'll be there to greet me when it's my turn to go home. I consider John one of my 'Joy' guides.

The yodeling and someone whose name began with 'S' never did register with me, and I have to remember to ask my mother if she can shed any light on that.

Claudette was absolutely on when talking about my mother. Mom is very alert. Her mind is sharp, but her body is slowly giving out. It looks so frail. I'm always amazed at how resilient she is. Most days when I talk to her, she still says she'd be quite happy to just go in her sleep. She has had just about every health problem you can get in one lifetime from stomach ulcers to breast cancer, and she's come through them all. I'll be honest; I never thought she would make it to her eighties never mind her nineties. I believe if it wasn't for her watercolour paintings (which are fantastic) she would have given up long ago. Claudette felt five more years for mom, and it wasn't far off at four. She passed peaceably in her sleep, just the way she wanted.

I was very happy that Lisa came through, and I've already written of my father-in-law.

It was interesting that my grandfather came through. As I said, I've never met him, and am not sure why he would come through, unless it was just to say hello, because he passed before I was born. My mother tells me he was a wonderful man.

I have seen pictures of him in his uniform. He was career Army, and definitely had the legging look that Claudette described.

My last question about our dog Toby was more out of curiosity than anything else, so I was pleasantly surprised when he finally showed up. I was also thrilled that Buster was there right away. He had been a badly abused dog that my father had picked up at the S.P.C.A. For the first few days he was very jumpy and would growl if you came near while he was eating. But once he saw we meant him no harm, he turned completely around and was devoted to all of us; a member of the family as though he'd always been there.

At that time, we were living in the country, so he was seldom tied up. We had a good size field behind our house which gave him lots of room to run. His only problem was that he loved to chase cars which was his undoing. He was with us only a few years when he got hit and killed. No matter how hard we tried to get him to stop, he just had to chase those cars. I was sick for weeks. Claudette was right again, he was more than a friend. I'm glad he showed up.

Toby lived a good life and was the smartest dog I've run across. We never had any real problems with him, except for the last few years. He became diabetic and had to have a shot every day. It still makes us laugh when we think about it. We'd say "Toby, come get your shot", and he would amble in and turn around, and we knew the only reason he would do it was because he got a treat. We got him as a puppy, and had him for twelve years. He became ill one day, and that evening we decided we'd better go to the emergency vet. He died in my arms just as we got there. Another sad few days. I'm glad the two of them are together.

I couldn't be happier with the way the reading went. I do feel like I'm going into a new part of my life. I will definitely do this again.

K. was very interested in what took place when I got back to work on Monday. I told him most of what happened. I think he would like to try it, but he seems hesitant. I think it may have something to do with his religious upbringing.

For the next several months not a lot changed for me. K. loaned me the rest of the *CWG* books by Neale Donald Walsch which I loved reading. One day I will get them for myself so I can reread them. The books that I would recommend to anyone interested are *Book I; Book III; Home with God;* and his latest *Happier than God.* I have read the first three books a couple of times.

I was still scraping by with good months and not so good. I tried to get down to Birch Bay whenever I could. I really enjoy my time there. Even two days feels like a nice break. It's very peaceful and there's a country setting with lots of farms when you get away from the water. For me, there's nothing like my early morning walks through the State Park, along the waterfront and back around to Beachwood. My daily meditations, which I look forward to, seem extra special there. They seem to fly by. I use Bill Harris's *Centrepointe* tapes for my meditations which last one hour, and for me the morning seems best.

So, this is the way it was going for me. It's now coming up to one year since my reading with Claudette. As I stated, I've continued my reading, meditating, and putting into practice a lot of what I have learned. Obviously, the one place I would like to see myself is in better financial shape. I'm doing my daily affirmations, and picturing myself as a healthy person with money, doing what I want to be doing. It's very easy to slip when things take a bad turn, and I have to be diligent in catching myself from negative thoughts.

But now, through these wonderful books, it's more than just the money. I'm looking at myself. Like Dr. Wayne Dyer says in his *Power of Intentions*, I'm trying to be better today than I was yesterday.

There are a lot of little things we can do for other people every day, like holding the door open for everyone, smiling, and wishing people a good day, which actually makes me feel better about my day. And as God says in the *CWG* books, when we help others, we're actually helping ourselves. What we do to others, we do to our self.

Overall, I would consider myself to have been a good person. But, as I'm sure we all can, I can look back and know I've done some pretty stupid and hurtful things, especially in my younger years when it was all fun and games, drinking and partying. I will gladly apologize to anyone I have slighted or to those whose feelings I was uncaring about at the time. It's hard for me to see myself now as that young, the hell-with-it kind of person. Having said that, I realize that all of it was necessary in getting me to where I am now. I had to go through those transitions to become the person I am at this moment.

We are ever-changing, and let me say right now, thank you to everyone who has been a part of my world, even the smallest of relationships, or meetings has helped me to get me to this spot.

It's now May, 2007 and I've decided to call Claudette for another reading. We set up an appointment for May 23rd. Once again I focus on who I would like to come through. I want to hear from John, and I'm hoping to get more information from my spirit guide Arthur. Also, it would be nice to get some idea of my financial situation.

I get to Claudette's at the designated time. It's pretty much like last time, and being there brings it all back to me. I'm excited to get going. Claudette comes from the back room and greets me warmly. She goes through the same procedures ----- the tape recorder is there and the prayer is said. I'm ready.

SECOND SESSION

May 23, 2007.

Claudette: "As I was saying my prayers, I was hearing 'How come you haven't got on with it? Just get on with it.' So I feel that you are in the process of postponing something that you should be doing."

Mike: "Oh, really."

Claudette: "So, I feel that you've had the opportunity to move forward and you keep putting on the brakes. Like saying, 'I'm not too sure. I don't know if I should. It's too risky.' or whatever. And I feel that we are talking about the totality. May I ask how old you are?"

Mike: "I just turned 60."

Claudette: "Perfect. So, when you were 59, you moved into your 60th year. With that, you just moved into a whole new 6 year increment that may throw you off balance a bit. Do you understand? Because things are no longer the same. They don't look the same. What used to look red now looks orange."

Mike: "I think I've made huge strides since a year ago. I've done so much reading, studying, and meditating, practicing and that. I just thought … ."

Claudette: "I don't mean that it's negative. What I'm saying is that as you moved into that year, that 60th, which makes what you said confirmation of what I was saying. Alright? So, life change. There was a whole new perspective on life. And I want to say that from 60 to 66, or 59 to 65, you are re-evaluating, re-establishing, and settling in to who you really want to be, and the poop with the rest of the world. I'm doing what I want to do. And, it's like you've dedicated your whole life in trying to, you know, promote this one, do that for this one, etc. etc. and basically putting yourself on the back burner. The other thing is that as you've been doing all your reading, meditating, it's also brought on some doubts. Um mm, it's like 'I'm not too sure. Well-ll, maybe. I don't know if I'm ….' It's all brought in this sense of insecurity, because you're into a whole different environment. See what I'm saying? And so, I want to say that I see one, two, three….I see three very strong influences around you from the spirit world. And I feel that these are guides and teachers, and one, I really feel that one is a protector. I feel that you are one who would not be stopped by mankind to get somewhere. If you make up your mind, 'I'm doing this', you're not going to let anyone stop you. And I feel that this….*yes, thank you*… that this is a spirit guardian that is with you, to help you not to be foolish, but at the same time not to stop you from your studies, as your saying…."

Mike: "I'm tingling all over right now."

Claudette: "Yes, yes. There's confirmation here. I want to say the other two are teachers. They're teaching you, and when you know you get that sense, that feeling, 'I should be doing this, but I can't be bothered.' Do it anyway. Okay? That 'I can't be bothered', or 'I'm too tired', is the personality that is putting in resistance blocks."

Mike: "I think that when I was here last time, you said that there was the name 'Arthur'. I don't know if that is one of the spirit guides."

Claudette: "Okay. Thank you. I'm hearing that Arthur is only going to be with you for another year. ('Oh'). And that this other….you're moving forward, and that you really have to get into the practical, the practicum of what you want to be. It's now time to try to feel where you want to be, and how to do that, and to pick and choose your teachers from the physical world, because the teachers from the spirit world have already chosen you. We don't choose them. They choose us. They chose you based on where you're at, and remember that a teacher has been observing you for seven years, before they actually demonstrate themselves. Okay?

('Okay') And I really feel that ….as I'm looking at these wonderful beings, I just said 'we know one is Arthur, who is the next one?' And, I just got 'Jack. Jack of all trades'. So, I feel that this other one has a real sense of humor, and that he needs to have a sense of humor to get you to do the work. Remember that you get the information on the 'need to know basis.' And the more that you can demonstrate that you are committed, that you are willing, the more that things will evolve. We are heading for a really accelerated time, and I feel that in the last year, you have demonstrated that, 'Okay, I'm willing, at least I'm willing, but I won't be totally blind', which is a good thing, because spirit does not want a puppet. They want somebody who can think, and has character, and who can stand strong. Not be foolish, but stand strong. Alright? So you're not as skeptical as you used to be. ('No, not a bit'). No, but it's good to have some skepticism, and to say 'ah, well, you know that's a little fishy. Show me.' Or always say 'Show me the reality.' because we have a personality, and our personalities get involved at times, so the thing to say is 'Show me the reality' not what I want to see or hear.

Claudette: "I also have ….*yes, thank you* … I also have a lady here that presented herself, and I want to say that she's a motherly vibration, and this lady has a ….it's not a tall person, and she comes with a great deal of love, and also an apple pie. (Laughing). She has an apple pie in her hand and I feel she would have loved to make pies – fruit pies. Do you have a grandmother type vibration that would have been short, please? Short. You're a tall man.

Mike: "There's two I can think of. One would either be my grandmother or my mother-in-law. They were short."

Claudette: "Okay. I feel … uh … I'm getting cold now. I want to say that I feel that this one … let me just say that she has a sense of humor, she has a smile, she has twinkly eyes when she just knows you're up to something. She could always know when you were up to something. Would this be your grandmother, please? ('That would be my grandmother.') Yes, and did they have an apple orchard or something? ('Um, not that I know.') Okay. So it's like I'm seeing big baskets of apples. She's coming in with that smirk on her face saying … say again … you're up for some wonderful adventures. ('Oh good'). She's coming in with that encouragement. Don't give up. Keep moving forward. And, I also want to say that she … *okay* … she says 'thank you for being you, and being there for me' because I feel that you were there for her at a very significant time in her life. ('Okay'). That she needed assistance and that you were able to give her that….not live with her, but give her that assistance. Would you understand what she was talking about? ('Yes, a little bit'). You would have been much younger. Early twenties. I get twenty-four with this.

('Twenty-four?'). Do you remember where you were at twenty-four? What was going on in her life? Was she still in the living at that time? ('No'). No, she was in spirit. ('Yes, definitely'). So, okay, twenty-four. What was happening at twenty-four?

Mike: "I have to tell you some of my twenties were vague. (Laughing).

Claudette: "Yeah, yeah, well. (Laughing). Then if you weren't there, she was there for you. ('That could be'). I feel that she would have gotten you out of situations. ('Okay, that would make more sense'). That would be the influence. So, it's a reverse thing here. But, she says 'thank you for trusting and believing in me'. Somehow it was her way of payback time that there was something that you did for her when she was in the living, and I feel that when she saw you in situations, let me put it that way, that she would have been around to guide you, to encourage you to the right direction.

Mike: "Sometimes these make more sense later on when I'm listening to them."

Claudette: "Okay. Alright then. Would you have been a teenager when she passed away?

Mike: "Um, just prior to teenager, I think. I remember my mom crying when she heard. I think I was about nine or ten. Unless this is somebody else I'm not getting..."

Claudette: "No. I still feel it's grandmother. This is such a loving, motherly type vibration. And, I really feel that whatever encounter you have had with her, she's saying 'thank you for being there for me.' You would have been the apple (apple pies?) of her eye, you know that kind of thing, and really brought her joy….joy every time that she would see you. Because you were quite the character, she says…. quite the character. She just enjoyed your spunk, as well, because you were 'very spunky' is how she says it. Very spunky. And the regret is that she wasn't here longer. She feels that if she had been here longer, maybe you wouldn't have gone through what you went through. You were rebellious. She says you were rebellious. You didn't like...didn't like the control that the adults had over you. But she had her way, that you just enjoyed. And so, anyways, this is what she's telling me. Then, she also says that you are...I'm getting the word...your spirit, your spiritual self is growing stronger and stronger, and it's not to separate the two, but to bring the two as one. And she says.....do you have a bible, please, because she's showing me a missal, or a bible, a prayer book of some kind?

Mike: "We did have a family bible. I remember it quite well, actually."

Claudette: "Okay. Do you know who has that? You don't have it?"

Mike: "No. My sister's got it now."

Claudette: "There are a few passages in this bible that she would love you to read. Not to become a bible reader, but rather that you would find inspiring, and if your sister doesn't mind, maybe she could lend it to you for a period of time, just to kind of .....as grandmother comes close to you, she will indicate which passage, because I feel that you are inspired, for the most part. All that you're reading is confirmation of the inspiration that you are getting." ('Okay') "And I also feel that you are in training, and the next 5 years will be continuous training, so be open to the event... be open to the various adventures or the direction, because it will keep changing. Do you understand, please?" ('Yes.') "Are you presently retired, or do you still have a business?"

Mike: "No, I'm still working."

Claudette: "Do you have your own business?"

Mike: "Well, it's sort of like my own business. I work at a company, but it's for myself really."

Claudette: "Okay. I want to say that gradually you'll be weaning yourself away from that as you get more into what it is that you are doing. But, I don't see that happening until you're 65ish, around there. But, gradually you're weaning yourself away from the 40 hour overdose of work, because you're moving into a higher frequency. Also, you will get a lot of tired periods when you'll say 'Why am I getting tired? I shouldn't be tired.' And that's the shift of energy, because as your energy shifts and changes, you'll need more rest until it is fully in frequency, because every adjustment when you rest, then they're able to adjust you much better."

"I also have a gentleman coming forward which I don't….your dad is in spirit is he not?" ('Yes'). And…, *yes thank you*….he would have been a tall man?

('Yes'). And he has a brother, please….a brother in spirit? ('Yes'). I feel that there are two of them here, and I first saw the uncle, and then your father showed up, and again, I feel that there's a very square jaw here, a very tight jaw. Would this be dad, please? ('Yes'). Very authoritative? ('Yes'). Military almost? ('Yes'). Was he in the military? ('Yes'). Thank you. Alright, because there's a very stern individual, but then he just relaxes, and he says 'I have so mellowed, and I have learned so many things' and he says 'boy oh boy, was I wrong.' (Claudette laughing) "He's coming to admit it, and it takes a lot for him to do that. Right? And the brother is kind of tapping him on the back, 'Good boy, good boy', (Claudette laughing) that sort of thing, because they were very different in personalities."

Mike: "I didn't know that uncle very well."

Claudette: "Okay, because there was quite a bit of difference, the sense I get is that one was more humorous, and the other one was sterner, and you ended up with the father who was stern, and I feel that that's the father you chose for the very journey you had to take. Do you understand, please? ('Yes'). Because now you go back and say 'I should have listened', but you had that rebelliousness.

(I have to say that my father had a great sense of humour, and had mellowed out quite a bit in his later years, but you sure didn't want to get on his bad side. That rebellious streak that Claudette mentioned got me in big trouble when I was younger on a number of occasions. You definitely wanted to do things dad's way, if you wanted to keep peace in the family, and my mother negotiated on my behalf many times.)

"I feel that you would have felt your oats very young in life. (My parents separated when I was eighteen, and eventually divorced. I moved out when they separated, because there was just not enough room. I moved in with three other guys, but that's a whole other book.) You rebelled very young in life, and it kept going until you were 36 or 35, your mid thirties when you said 'Whoa, I better do something here' that sort of thing. Since then, you've really been doing, doing, doing, and trying to establish, to improve yourself, and demonstrate that you are a responsible individual. You know what happened, you were born with sensitivity; because of the work you need to do, and I want to say the next 20 years is where the spirit work comes in. So, you've been in training through all this rebellion and all this to show you how really strong you are, and to heal the scars that were left in you."

"As you move into….you're heading for why you are here. Be prepared to wean yourself away from the norm, yet we don't want…again I want to say, and I'll say it again and again, we don't separate our self from the physical world, you can't be up there in la la land, because you're here on earth to do a job. Do you understand?" ('Yes') "That job is not to be shown until you are ready. You have been in training since you were born. You've been very sensitive and clairvoyant as well, and it's the clairvoyance that scared the poop out of you." ('Yes, definitely'). "Yeah, yeah, and it's accepting who you are, as normal. Your clairvoyance, your sensitivity, that's the norm for you. You have to accept that, and embrace that and the more you do, the more everything will be shown to you."

"Um, yes…have you been writing please? Have you been writing?" ('Not really, no'). "I'm seeing you write. So if you haven't been doing it, then this will part of the discipline….is sit down and write."

Mike: "You told me to do that the last time, to write when I was meditating…to write when thoughts came into my head, but it interfered with my meditation, so I sort of started it and then I stopped."

Claudette: "You have to do it at the end…. ('Yes, okay')…. not during the meditation, but at the end, and if you don't remember, you ask your spirit guides to give you a review, because anything that occurred, you have access to. Do you understand, please?"

('Yes'). "What has not happened is subject to change. What has happened, you can always tap back into it…always, always; because you are psychic, you have the ability. Yes, you need to start journaling, and I'm sorry if you misunderstood me, it's not during meditation, but always after, because it brings you too much back to earth and you'll lose it. Or even have a recorder, if you don't want to write, just record, the information will come through. I also see you writing a book." ('Really?') "I really feel that there's a part of you that is going to do some written words... the written word is the way I'm getting it."

"Um...two, three...I feel there are about 3 steps, and each represents a guide, and the sense that I get is each step is a 2 year period. And so when I said Arthur is there for you, that makes sense now. He's there for another year, and that's his 2 years, and then you move to the next guide who is 2 years, and the next guy... but you also have a band, or a circle of guides. That again, the more you are in readiness, the more that you will be shown this. The band is where you have your regular guide plus experts in various areas that you're going to be working with. And I really feel that the next four years....by four years you will be in readiness to do what you've come to do, because the world is changing, the energies are changing, and you are in acceleration now, so you're going to move from one thing to the other, to the other, and you just have to make time for it. You can't allow yourself to be deterred from that. Okay? You still have to support yourself, you still have to work, but that's going to slow down, and you're going to have enough financial means to support yourself and do the work at the same time."

"So, I feel that you are also a healer, please? I understand that you are a healer, and this again will prove itself."

Mike: "I've been trying to work on that. Like sending out vibrations to people that I know are unwell. (My good friends Dick & Marilyn both had cancer. I had been trying to send out healing energies to them. Unfortunately, both succumbed to the disease – Dick had passed six weeks prior to this session, and I will try to contact him later in this session. Marilyn passed about eight months later. They are both dearly missed. I am still working on this though with others who are having health issues.)

Claudette: "Distant healing. Yes, distant healing. You just make a list and take one day a week where you just sit, and you can do it as a group if you don't have time, but you just name....say the meditation, and you bring in the source, the healing energy, and you say 'I'd like to send a healing energy to...' and you just read the names. Just do it once a week. That way you then look forward to it and it's not taking all of your time. So, you shouldn't have more than half an hour, otherwise you'll just postpone it, and put it off. But you are a healer, and that will demonstrate itself more and more to you."

"Are you presently in a relationship, please? ('No'). Okay, because I feel that your partner….that there's a partnership coming in here, as in relationship, not so much as in business partner. I want to say a relationship, a romantic type, and even though you're skeptical about these things, I feel that as you shift and change your energies, you will draw to you the personality or energy that will compliment, do you understand? So, it's about being two very different energies, and yet being a team…. ('Okay')

…and respecting and honouring the differences; let's agree to be different, let's agree to disagree, you are you and let's have fun, and it's no fun to have the same all the time, we get bored." ('Okay').

"So, I feel that this relationship coming in will stimulate parts of you that have been dormant, or that you haven't activated and vice-verse, you'll be able to do the same; so that there is a nice compliment, and yet you're very independent. You need that independence. You cannot have a relationship that is co-dependent, there's not time for that anymore, nor can you be co-dependent on someone else…. ('Right') ….and it's just not to be, it's time to move on, because there is a lot of wonderful work to be done, and we need partners to kind of support and just be there… be in the same house, the same room, or whatever, you have to hear them talk, have them around, so we don't feel so alone, and the other thing about spiritual work…. when we are working with our spirit, on the spirit level it's very lonely. No matter how many friends we have, it's a lonely job. It's nice to have that support. Even though there are many people who have partners that are spiritual, etc. it still lonely, because that soul is still thirsting for that home, and it's not on this earth plane, so the thing that you need to know very clearly, is that this earth journey is very temporary, it doesn't mean you're going to die tomorrow, no, no, you've got a lot of time, be ready for the long term, and I want to say that your health will serve you well." ('Okay').

"… Sorry, I lost it when I got into the health,… *can you bring it back please*? What was I saying before the health thing? ('Relationship?') We were into the relationship, okay, moving into the long term, the soul journey being demonstrated to you, the purpose of your life, etc."

"Okay, let's go to the questions, and if it comes back…you'll have it on the tape anyway."

Mike: "I was hoping my…the last time I was here …. when I was younger, right around when I was 24 or so, the girl I was with had an abortion and you said that this child came through, and I had to give him a name, which I did, and I was hoping…I just wanted to say hello to John."

Claudette: "Boy". ('Yes, boy'). "As you said this, a young man manifested himself, and I'm getting a lot of confirmation here. There's a nice smile and contentment with him, so he's really pleased that you have been communicating, and he says (Claudette laughing) sometimes you are very stubborn. He's been trying to get a point across to you, and you're not listening, do you understand, please? ('I don't know'). You don't know what he's talking about? Okay, do you have a home, a house?" ('No, an apartment, and I have a place down at Birch Bay that I go to most weekends').

"Now, do you have a garden there?" ('Yes'). "And, have you been doing your gardening?" ('A little bit, yes'). "A little bit, because I feel it has to do with a garden. So, he's been trying to get you to set up your garden a certain way that you can do your meditations, do you know what I mean?"

Mike: 'It's been on my mind."

Claudette: "AHA! (Laughing). That's what he's been trying to get across to you, and you keep putting it off, and putting it off. Yes, okay, that's where that inspiration in regards to the garden, has also been from him, and it's just about how to do it in such a way that you have vibration, okay? I feel that there's a spot in your… on your land, that's a vortex, there's an energy spot there. If you could please, just walk about slowly, feel, and you'll get that shiver up and down your back. Just walk slowly, that's your meditation spot. ('Okay'). This is a connection from the core of the earth, all the way to Source… ('Oh')…. and it's going to be very beneficial, so that you can expedite your development. So your clairvoyance,… because you've kind of pushed it to the back burner,… is a little foggy right now, yes? And, it just needs clarity and I feel that energy will just clear it up."

Mike: "I've been trying to work on that, like hoping that somebody would come through, but it hasn't really been working too much."

Claudette: "What, the clairvoyance?"

Mike: "Yes. Like years ago, I heard a voice as clear as a bell, and it scared me at the time, and I've been hoping that would happen again, and it hasn't."

Claudette: "But what that indicates though, is that you have the ability to be a clairaudient … ('Right') … .that means that you will hear spirit. All you need to do now is just trust that it will come; so you work with your strongest ones (spirit guides) first, and everything will fall together."

"Where do you live?"

Mike: "Right now, I'm in Marpole." (area in Vancouver)

Claudette: "Yes, because we do have development classes here, you know that, eh?"

Mike: "Yes, I should do that."

Claudette: "Just think about that. Now, let's go on."

Mike: "The other thing is, I had a very close friend, one of my best friends, pass about six weeks ago. ('Okay'). His name was Dick, and I didn't know if he might come through?"

Claudette: "Was he a salesman?"

Mike: "No. He was retired but …"

Claudette: "I have a gentleman … I haven't seen Dick yet, but I have a Jim, James … the letter 'J' please. Would there have been a salesperson, salesman that you would have known … I want to go when you were in your late twenties, early thirties? Because, as you mentioned your friend who had passed away, there was this other 'friendship' tie, and I feel that he would have been at the time a drinker, somebody who would have drank a lot. ('Yes'). And… ('Kim?') … I got 'im'; I thought it was 'Jim', but anyway…"

Mike: "There was a friend of mine, right around there that died from drinking."

Claudette: "Yes. I just got confirmation. He was a salesperson, was he?" ('Sort of'). He just showed right up, as soon as you said friend… poof, there he was. And, he would have passed away around that time. ('Yes'). Okay, and he would have had a sense of humour as well…. ('Oh yes') …. a real daredevil type of individual. ('Yes'). (Claudette laughing). Yes, if you had given him a horse, he would have rode it down the street, saying 'yahoo, cowboy'. (Still laughing). He's definitely coming in with that crazy sense of humor But he's also saying that since he's been in spirit, he went to rehabilitation." (Laughing).

"It's a very different world." He says. "You should have seen me when I crossed over. 'Where am I?'" He's saying, 'What am I doing here?' It was a real shocker. Like 'Huh? What am I doing…?"

"It took him a long time to adapt. A long time in earth years, but not so long on the other side, because there's no time, right? ('Yes'). What he comes to say is that 'in my rehabilitation, I have learned a lot, and I've gone to the 'Hall of Learning'. And, he says 'I'm going to do my work on the other side."

"*Yes… thank you…* And he says he's going to help the masses that cross over.

They are readying. They're getting themselves prepared for that, because there's going to be a lot coming.* Do you understand, please? So, he says 'I'd love to work with you…' ('Great') … work as partners, because you already know each other. But, he says 'I still have a lot to learn, and I'm not a guide, I would be a helper. Just call on me and I will try and help, but it doesn't mean that I have all the answers.' 'The point that he's trying to make is that they're really getting ready for mass crossings,* there's something that's about to happen, that will ….. you know you're here, he says, to rebuild, you're here on the earth plane, is what he's saying, you're here to rebuild the new world.' Do you understand, please?' ('Okay'). And, he says that means getting rid of the old paradigms, and the old habits."

*(Could he be referring to the cyclone which hit Myanmar in May, 2008 which killed 138,366 and the disastrous earthquake in Haiti in 2010 which claimed approximately 160,000 lives?)

"As you look at things from a new perspective, and because you're working with the spirit world, be ready for some things that don't make sense. Because we're trying to make sense with the physical mind and it doesn't always connect, and we put it on the shelf until spirit proves himself."

"Now, he's saying that your friend that passed away six weeks ago is adapting much better than he did, but he's still not ready to communicate, alright? But I feel.... did he have a chest condition?' ('Yes'). 'I'm having trouble breathing.' ('Yes, definitely'). 'Okay, thank you, so he says he's still ..... oh, wait a minute here he comes, and he's coming in with two what I would call male nurses, because he's presenting himself in that hospital look.' ('Yes, he was very sick before he died in the hospital.') 'He... *yes thank you*...... I'm having trouble breathing here, and he says.. 'Just look at me now, I can breathe, and I feel so good.' 'He says I'm still healing but it won't be long. Six weeks on earth is like six seconds here."

" He has made it through that transition, and now he's reviewing and going over things, and he says ' I'll be around, don't you worry.' " So, he's fine, he did make it across, and he's adapting, and he's getting his ...... when you cross over, you go through a review of your life, and then based on that, you go wherever, and so he says ' I'm soon to get my directions. (Claudette laughing) I haven't got them yet. Whoa. I can't wait to see what that will be.' ('Sounds just like him.') " So he's just got that look. (Claudette laughing). 'So, lots of love and again appreciation for you, and gratitude... thank you...thank you for being there, and doing what you did, whatever that was... and this other guy... Kim...and he's saying ' you know if it hadn't been for you a few times, I think I would have been dead, and I thank you again for that,' so he says ' now it's payback time, I'm here to help, just call on me.'" ('Wonderful').

"So, right away your son came in, because we're about to close, and your son came in and he says, ' You know, dad, we're doing good, we're doing good. He says ' not to worry, you worry too much. Don't worry so much.' And, he says ' I'll help you find that woman. '" (Both of us laughing).

Mike: " Good for you."

Claudette: "He says, ' as much as you are busy... you would love to have the perfect companionship', and that's part of your desire. The bottom line, Mike, is that you want to be loved.. you see.. in the correct way, and not with this.. ' oh, whatever '. And may I say to you that within the next few years, it's there to be had... it's there. That frequency is so strong...it's there to be had. You've got guides there to work with you....you may need to locate some kind of physical teacher to work with you, whatever that takes, your guides will direct you....they will direct you on what to do. Please sit in meditation with your guides... probably in that nice spot of yours, that garden that you're working on, and just say ' alright what should I do about this? Do you feel that this is where I need to go... blah, blah, blah, blah.'"

"Because I feel that you have some ideas in your mind, and that you just need to get confirmation from your own guides.. because I feel that your guidance will come from that higher guidance.. that you need to be able to connect to that... really that's where your next four years are.. to get a hold of that link, and never break that link. It doesn't matter which guide it is, you still need that link to higher guidance, because you will need ...at the moment of chaotic world.. to rebuild, because then you will need to know where.... and I also see you working with young adults and children for some reason in a teaching capacity.. so I feel that's down the road. And, please don't look at age as a problem, because the more you get into your spirit self and the work that you do, the younger you get.. the age is not going to be a detriment. Last question and we're done."

Mike: "Um, the last question is... I've had this thought of this dream house of mine, that I would love to build, and I believe that it's going to happen, but I'm just wondering if you see anything coming along?"

Claudette: " You've got a two year period that you need to work through, because a dream house will need to be in the right location, and I feel that won't happen for another two years, because there's too much happening right now and there's going to be closure, remember this year is the year of closure, okay? And you close old doors, and you open new ones, and put your money away, and just know it's going to happen, but you're also going to need the network of people that are going to help you build or create the environment, and I see it more of an estate, like a British estate versus a ranch house or as much as you would like a ranch house you are going to get

... ('It was more of a farm house'). **Claudette: ...** Ranch. Farm.. (laughing)

What I'm seeing is... I'm seeing an estate which is very much as an educational centre... so you need a large place, and then you have your little, what I would say is a gardener's cottage... so you've got the big estate, and the cottage where you live, and that estate becomes the educational group, whatever, and you could have boarding school, boarding for adults and children. So just know that there's all kinds of possibilities, and the way you envision now is only a little piece of it... so that will get bigger and bigger as you get more receptive. You know how to ground yourself? Right? Grounding is so that you are able to receive the data."

Mike: "That's like cleansing and..."

Claudette: "No, grounding is like .. you know when you ground a socket? ('Yes'). Because it's haywire, right? It doesn't funnel through properly. Same with you. Grounding is so that the information, and the data, the electrical data, because it's all electricity... (Energy)... it's funneled through, so think of yourself as a socket.... the grounding is where you send roots down to the core of the earth."

Mike: "Right. I think I remember reading that somewhere."

Claudette: "Yes. Most people say it's so you can find your body again, or that you don't Astral Travel. What it is, is that you can have that funneling...so that the light can come in, the energy can come in, the data can come in... just think of the socket, it's the same thing. And, the other thing is that when you do Astral Travel, when you do leave, it's a beacon to get you back in proper.. we always get back, because we're tied with our *Silver Cord*, but what it does is bring you properly. This is your homing device, as well. So, it's a multitasking. I'll leave that with you, and say God bless."

Mike: "Thank you very much."

Okay. Another interesting session.

When Claudette was speaking of the guides, I got a tingling sensation all over. I believe and know now that this is a connection with spirit. It has happened to me during several meditations, if I think of a particular person. It also happens occasionally when I'm reading these transcripts, most recently when reading and then thinking of my grandmother. I tingled all over and then said ' Hi, nanny. Thanks for being here and saying hello. '

My grandmother is right there, and again I only knew her when I was young. So, she was long passed when I was in my twenties. But, I can see that as a reverse thing, and her wanting to be of assistance to me in my twenties, because there were definitely situations that I got myself into in those years. I did rebel against adults at a young age, when she was living with us. I don't remember now what it was exactly. I was around five, and something I wanted to do or have, and my father said no. So, I packed up a few belongings in a scarf, or towel, and told my parents I was leaving and going to live with my uncle George, who was doing some work in Seattle at the time. We were living on Long Island, New York. Off I went. I didn't go too far though. I'd been gone maybe half an hour and it was already getting dark when I left, and my mom and nanny were getting worried. She asked dad if they should go looking for me. He said ' No, he'll be back. ' And, not too long after that I was. Dad asked me why I was back, and I said it was too dark and I'll leave in the morning. Of course that was the end of it, and nothing more was mentioned.

I was glad John came through. I must get that stubbornness from my dad that he's talking about, when he's trying to get that point across to me.

It was good to hear from my friend Kim. He was also in the brokerage industry and worked on the floor of the Exchange. He did have a problem with alcohol though, which cost him his job, his marriage, and eventually his life. I ran into him a couple of months after he lost his job and he told me he had cleaned up his act, and would really like to get back to work. I actually needed someone at the time, and said I would hire him if he promised to keep away from the booze. He was good for a few months, but then I started noticing that part way through the day, it looked as though he would stagger a bit, and his face looked flushed. I confronted him about it, but he said no, he was okay. This went on for a couple of weeks. I had my suspicions but could never find where he was hiding it. Alcoholics can be ingenious in stashing there supplies. One day I happened to walk into a bar I didn't normally frequent when I saw Kim with a couple of beers. I asked him what was going on, and he said ' it's only beer, I can handle it.' I knew he was back on the alcohol, and then it got worse at work. Eventually I had to let him go. Not long after, I heard his parents came out from the east, where he was originally from and brought him home. It was maybe a year later that I heard he had been found downtown in an ally dead. I can understand his surprise when he crossed over. Suddenly you're in a whole other place, like ' what's going on?'. He was a good guy with a bad problem. We had a lot of good times together. I appreciate the kind words, and I'm glad he's going to be there for me.

Kim has decided to do his progression on the other side now. I've read that some souls find the earthly experience to be too much for them, so they decide not to reincarnate, but to move forward doing their work in an easier environment.

When we decide to take on this existence, we set certain tests that we wish to experience. We can set this bar pretty high when in the non-physical, usually against the advice of our spirit guides. Upon joining this physical plane, and when these barriers or contrasts start appearing, they can be much more daunting than we imagined in the non-physical. At my low point when getting bombarded with constant troubling situations, I didn't handle it well at all. Fortunately, I managed to get through it with a lot of help from here and the other side.

It was also nice that my good friend Dick came through. Although I couldn't hear him, it did sound like him, when Claudette passed on his comments. He was a good person, so his 'life review' should go well.

It's always good to hear from my dad.

The relationship part was interesting and also the bit about the educational center.

There's lots of information for me to think about.

Three years have gone by, and I feel like it's time to meet with Claudette again.

THIRD SESSION

Claudette: "This is June 11, 2010."

"As I'm saying the prayer, I'm becoming aware of a gentleman, that is here, that came in... but I keep hearing the name Paul.. Paul.. do you have a Paul in spirit, please? Somebody that you know, a friendship tie in spirit, please, by the name of Paul?"

Mike: "Hmmm. Oh, well when I was a kid..."

Claudette: "I got confirmation, oh I should say I got confirmation right away."

Mike: "When I was a kid there was a Paul.... Paul... ummm."

Claudette: "Somebody that ... it was definitely a friendship.. a tie.. somebody that you would have been friends with, etc. And, I feel that I have a throat condition with him, and a chest condition, and.... *give me something please*... you played with marbles when you were a child?"

Mike: "This would be.. you know what happened was .. and I heard about this after I moved away from back East, that this fellow had a bad relationship with somebody and wound up hanging himself."

Claudette: "Okay.. *thank you...yes, thank you.* Right, this is Paul right here."

Mike: : "Okay, I just got a tingling going through my whole self."

Claudette: "Yeah, yeah. There you go. So, Paul is here ...and he (laughing) he says ' you stole my marbles… ('Oh, really?')… whatever that means. So you must have had marbles... days when you played marbles."

Mike: "I don't remember that. Okay."

Claudette: "So, he's says I'm not talking about up here. So, he says you're going to be hearing from the family, or someone, and he says you need to tell them that I'm okay, I've made it to spirit, and that I'm healing myself, and working, and rehabilitating... if you like.. so that he did make it across to the light, to the spirit world, and that he was greeted by his grandparents. And, that he's been nurtured, and healing, and opening up to a greater understanding, and so forth. ('Okay'). And, it was all his doing, of course, and that he just lost his way, perspective. .. yes, lost his way, and that no one in the family need to blame themselves. He's telling me that somebody in the family is blaming them self, and they have to say no it is not their fault, it was his journey, his drama, his thing, and that they must not blame them self."

"He's coming because you're here, and you need to pass that on to the family.

('Okay'). And he says that when you were young you were of great assistance to him. That you were a listening board for him, and you kind of bantered about, but there was a lot of help there as well. And, he says 'don't forget that you do help a lot of people, you just don't realize who you have touched, and you make a difference in people's lives'.... is what he's saying. Do you understand, please? ('Okay'). *Yes, thank you.*"

"Is your dad in spirit, as well? (' He is. '). I'm getting a father vibration... so here's a fellow, he's sticking around, he's standing right beside you, and I feel he's a tall gentleman, please? ('Yes'). And very...talks in a deeper voice.. ('Yes'). I feel very... when he's talking it feels like the energy's coming from way down here... like that very deep kind of voice... so that when he spoke everybody heard him.. ('Yep '). .. and paid attention because he had that authoritative voice. He says... (Claudette laughing) ... I was just a wuss in certain ways ... so he had a good facade. But, I feel that your dad was a very... he's telling me that he was very sensitive, but that it's not something that you show. So, he was sensitive, but he couldn't show it... so, he had this facade of .. rrrrrr... but deep down he was a softy. And so I see the two of you... nnnngnnnng ...going at each other ... do you understand, please? So, there was this barking at each other... ('Yes') ...sort of thing. But, he says I never doubted that you loved me, and please never doubt that I did love you. He says that ' you were too much like me'. (' Yes, I know that. '). And, he says that I come to let you know that, to say that you must look at what is your highest good, not what everybody else thinks, but what is your highest good, and sometimes it's not an easy decision. In your ... *yes, thank you* ... in your personal life, he's referring to personal life, you're hitting your head against the wall, and it's like ' I should '... he hears you say ' I should, I could, I would, ' you know all these things, and he says ' stop ', and ' what is it for my highest good? ', because as you are right now, you're stopping the progress, not only for yourself, but for everyone else around you, because in making the decision everybody else will find their way as well. Does that make sense, please?" (' Yes '). "Because you're afraid of hurting or harming. And I hear you've got to let it go, and to say 'where am I, what do I want ', and just go with that."

(' Okay ').

Claudette: "Are you in your mid fifties, please?"

Mike: "No, I'm sixty-three."

Claudette: "Sixty-three. So, you've got... Do you have a birthday coming up?"

Mike: "I just had one a couple of months ago."

Claudette: "So, you just turned sixty-three." (' Yes '). " So, you've got two more years of establishing yourself. Basically with you Mike, it's ' who am I, what do I want '. It's not about age here. It's a six year increment. I think we've covered that before. (' Yes '). And this is about empowering yourself, finding you, the real you, and actually living by who you really are, and not by all the expectations of everybody else around you. And, that's been difficult because at the same time, you are also sensitive, and you don't want to harm and hurt people, and whatever, but you have to stop, detach from the end result, and say that we come on each other's path, to grow together, and then we may go separate ways to grow. So, it's always this kind of thing that happens."

Mike: "Well, I kind of know where I want to be going, and everything else, it's just ... uh... I'm just not sure if I'm getting there fast enough or like you know ...".

Claudette: "Well, you can't cheat the process, see?" ('Yeah '). " That's the thing, and so when we want to get there, we have to make sure we do the foundation ... each step has to be secure."

Mike: "It just seems to be taking a long time with the same steps."

Claudette: "What are you talking about as far as your steps?"

Mike: "Well, I mean I've uh...."

Claudette: "Would you understand a Judy, or Julia in spirit, please?" ('No '). " Female, cousin, do you have a cousin in spirit?"

Mike: "No, well not as far as I know. I have some cousins in England, but I don't ..."

Claudette: "Anyways, go ahead, I'll wait."

Mike: "I'm just thinking, that I'm doing a lot of affirmations, meditations. I'm trying to increase my, ...uh...vibrational frequency, or increase my energy, my vibrational energy. I'm trying to bring this up and do things, uh...."

Claudette: "Okay, so let me tell you about affirmations, and one, we want to shift our vibrations, and so on, do you understand? Are you attending a development class, or anything?"

Mike: "No. I'm just reading a lot, and uh..."

Claudette: "Well, maybe you need to start thinking about that. Where do you live again?" ('Marpole, Vancouver, just over the bridge.') " We have a class on Wednesday's in Burnaby, which will change to Thursday in the fall. Uh...".

Mike: "Is that the Spiritual Church in Burnaby?"

Claudette: "Well, there is that one, but we're not having it at the Church. We're using one of the lady's offices, and there is one in Surrey. But, think about that." (' Okay. '). " Because you're at a point where you need coaching. And so, when you do affirmations, and what was the other thing you said?" (' Shifting...'). " Shifting your vibrations. You need what I would call the ' *Alchemist* 'to come in to work on your vibration and so on. You need to be part of a group, a group energy moves you faster, do you understand?" (' Yes, that makes sense. '). We're getting at the point of urgency for where we're going, what we need to do, etc. and so on. So consider that. It doesn't have to be with me. It could be with anybody. But, you need to get into a group, because the group energy can move you faster and forward, to identify your guides, to know who they are, to work with them, to the shift, and so on. If you do your affirmations intellectually, you're not going to get there. It's to feel it in your heart. If, you come from that heart vibration, you will create... you will manifest it. If you come from the intellect, you may not manifest it, or you will manifest the positive and the negative of it."

Mike: "I've been trying to switch that. I've been doing all of my stuff.. I think.. has been in my head. Lately, I've been trying to move it down, and get it from the heart."

Claudette: "Right, so again, it's about opening up the heart, and the way of the future is the way of the heart, do you understand? And, the communication with the spirit guides, teachers, whoever, is from the heart. Anything from the exquisite mind, the intellect, the physical mind is not going to get you anywhere. The physical mind is really to function in this world, but the actual manifestation, and vibration is to do with the heart, because that's where your soul is. So your power center for the physical is in your solar plexus, your power center for your spirit, for your soul is in your heart. And, that's where we need to communicate with God, with all Source, etc."

Mike: "Are there any spirit guides around... or coming through right now?"

(' With you? ') " Yes."

Claudette: "I see one, two, three.. and then I see another group behind. See, I've got the three there, and another group behind, and I hear ' now is the time

'... now is the time for you to commit yourself to development, if that's really what you want to do. And, sometimes when we do meditations alone, there's too many things that interfere, or we can't seem to move the vibration high enough. Right? And, that's why group, even if it's for six months or a year, whatever, to just... have the advantage of larger energy to shift you up, do you understand?" (' Yes, that makes sense. ') "So, that will... and since you have been doing your work, and the desire is there, and you're willing, then it's exhilarating." So, when we do it alone, it's just not enough, and we need all the assistance we can get at this particular time. I feel that your life is on the borderline of shifting more. But, it's about taking... *yes... yes*...um... just know that we never know the whole picture. We just get it on a need to know basis, right? And, if we keep an open mind, or our thought is, 'I'm heading in this area', but as you go through the process, you may end up over here. But, to be flexible enough to follow your intuition, etc." (' Right '). And so, you're presently married, please?"

Mike: "No, I've been separated for a number of years.. seven years."

Claudette: "Okay, .. um... I heard you're getting married. (Claudette laughing)."

Mike: "I don't even have a girlfriend. (Mike laughing)."

Claudette: "In time that will come."

Mike: "Actually, the last time I was here, you said I would meet somebody, and ah...when I was sixty, I think. I may have met them, but I never...ha ha... nothing ever happened."

Claudette: "It never went anywhere, and so on. Whatever the free will is of whomever, things can change. So, as we sit now, this is what it looks like, but that may change with the next step. And so... it's... I heard you are getting married. So, you will meet someone that will... that you will...how can I say... it's a vibration that will compliment you, and will have the same interest, and the two of you will become a team. You're independent, but you become a team. So, it's not co-dependency."

Mike: "Yes, you sort of mentioned that last time, too. That we would compliment each other or something."

Claudette: "Right. Well, it hasn't changed. It's still there in your vibration, because I don't make these things up." ('Yes. '). " We were talking about something else, and *whoop*, that kind of came in here."

Mike: "Does it say when, or...?"

Claudette: "Well you know again, time is not linear, right." ('Yes, right. '). " And so, it's all about the process, and I really feel that it's within the next few years, anyways, right? That there is going to be...so, you obviously haven't met the right person yet."

('Right '). " Otherwise it would have happened. When spirit says these things are going to happen, it's just about the timing, that's all, you know, like it can be a year, two years, whatever."

Mike: "I know my son... um...he ah... he said he was going to look out for someone for me." (Laughing.)

Claudette: (Laughing.). "Who was in spirit? Your son is in spirit?"

Mike: "He was ... ah...never born. ('Okay. '). " John... he wanted a name..." ('Good.')... " So, I gave him the name John."

Claudette: "Well, you know what, obviously, you weren't ready for it either. So, there's a process of shedding, so that you can be freer, and ready to share your time, and share your life with somebody. And, there's a part of you that still wants that independence, still wants that freedom... ('Yes')... that I don't want to be imposed, that kind of thing."

('That's true.'). " But, remember that this woman of the future for you, is not going to hold you like that. Because you come with that understanding, ' hey, wait a minute, we've been through a lot of poop'. Right? In other words, you have and she has, and you know what, we're not going to have this."

Mike: "No, I've changed my philosophy in that regard in a lot of ways."

Claudette: "And so, the other thing is if you're not a widower, then you have to look at your divorce. Because it's about closure, it's not just that, but it's about closure. And it's about setting both of you free to actually experience...as long as there's an anchor, there's interference. The fact that you're still married, for whatever reason...it's... it's time now. It's time to let it go, and move along, both of you. To just move on. That sort of thing."

"And...ah...*yes, thank you*... are you traveling east? I'm seeing a plane going east. Are you traveling east?" (' Not that I know of. '). " Keep your mind open. Put that on the shelf, because I see you traveling east, and I feel like there's a calling, or somebody calls. Or you're invited. But, you're not living there, you are traveling there." (' I've got cousins back there, so it could be something like that....'). " Yes, somebody's calling you up, and you're going on a visit of some kind."

"But, I also feel that you will go across the ocean, do you understand, please? I feel that you will travel across the ocean, and I feel... *yes, thank you*.... this is to do with your spiritual development, and that your guide will tell you when the right time is, either to go to a place like *Arthur Findlay College ,* or one of the other you know... the *ISF*...the *International Spiritual Federation*... whatever. Yes, all of those... they have different activities, different things going on, and ... but, I do see you exploring that, so I feel that..." (' That would be cool. '). "Yes, I feel the next two years is about exploring. Exploring these things. Visiting places like that. Going with a group. You don't have to be on your own, but going with a group of spiritual people, so that you can bounce off ideas, visions, sights, insights, whatever, and compare notes. So, it's a spiritual journey, not a romantic journey. So that you have that thing going on. And, I'm excited because...

ah ha's...so I'm hearing a lot of ... *ah ha's*... *ah ha*...you know what I'm saying? And it's like 'okay I've been meandering', and that's what you've been doing. Meandering." ('Right'). " Welllll....nah, nah, nah, nah. I want. I want. I want. But, then there's got to be action. Do you understand, please?" ('Yes'). "It's like, 'okay if I go there, then I can't do this.' And it's what's important to you."

"I also feel... you're not retired yet?" (' No. No, still working.'). " But, you will be soon?" ('Well, not the way things are going.'). (Both laughing.). " Well, ...I just feel ... that...that there's that desire of retirement." ('Well, there's definitely that.'). " And, I feel... ' Hang in there. Don't give up... and just ... trust...trust.' It's all about learning to trust, and believe that things will fall into place... to afford you, and give that freedom to explore greater than the physical world, right? And, this has been going on with you for quite a while... quite a while. ('Yes.'). And, I'm hearing the time is coming... the time is coming, Again, when spirit says it's around the corner, it could be a few years, do you understand, please? ('Yes.'). Because around the corner for them and for us, is two different things."

Mike: "Yes, I'm starting to get tired of the way things have been going. I don't seem to be progressing too far, you know with my personal area. It's just going on and on...nothing is changing. As much as I'm trying to make things better, whatever... I just seem to be rolling along with the same old things... so..."

Claudette: "But, there's no trauma. ('No, no trauma.') See? Look at what is working,.. and what is working is there's no trauma here. ('No.'). And so, it's like you're in waiting. It's like a loll... well, the loll is about to move forward here. Because we're also moving into a time where North America is going to be suffering as far as earth shifts, and things like that... so it's happening everywhere else. We're not going to be exempt. You know it's heading this way. So, we have to be in readiness, and part of that readiness is, have a clear, strong connection to higher guidance, right? And, this is where you need to hit... it's that purity, that challenge, you know? Where do you go for this? Well, you go where people are doing this. You find the teacher that you want...you find the person that can help you, that you feel that you can resonate with. Then you visit in our environment, ...well the spiritual structures, you visit all of them...you see who you feel a resonance with, and all of that sort of thing. ('Right'). And then, you find out more about their classes, and what they're doing... and so on. And so, it goes like this...and then you take steps. Then, when you have demonstrated that... then things start shifting more, and it changes your life. Doing the *GAPP* (Gratitude, Ascension, Protection, and Power of Intent. Claudette does a *GAPP* session with me at the end of the fourth session.) everyday will shift and change your life, because you're looking at life from a different perspective. Instead of being here, and wishing to be there... you are. Then, you're open to both worlds. What we need to learn, is to walk between the two worlds...in other-words, it's not that you're dead, it's just that you're aware of the physical, and you're aware of other dimensions, other frequencies." ('Definitely... I'm definitely aware of that.'). " We're not talking about just spirit... dead people, we're talking frequencies, other dimensions. Alright?" ('Yes. I have been looking into that.'). " And, this is what we need to do. That means you have to commit yourself on a weekly basis... minimum, because alone it's not enough. Now.. um....'.

Mike: "Is my mother..."?

Claudette: "Who...just a sec... who...um... I'm seeing... I'm looking and I'm seeing this lady, and then you said ' is my mother '. You're mother is in spirit, please?" (' Yes. '). " Was she a short lady, please?". (' So, so. '). " I see a short lady and she says, (Claudette laughing) ' sometimes I was sneaky ', does that make sense to you?" (' Ah, not really, no. '). " Okay... she's saying her voice was squeaky... there were times when her voice would go funny, does that make sense to you?" (' Ahhhh....not really. ').

" Okay, alright, let me find out. Who's Betty, or Beatrice... the letter B? ('Hmmmm.'). Would you understand a Marge... Margaret?" (' No. '). " Okay, so do you have an aunt, or great aunt in spirit?"

Mike: "I've got a few of them, but I never knew any of them."

Claudette: "Do you know if any of them would have that name?"

Mike: "They might have. They were all in England."

Claudette: "Was your mother from England? (' Yes. '). " Good. So, I feel that I have an auntie here, because as soon as I said auntie, I got mother's side of the family... like sister, mothers. (' Hmmm. ').

"So, even though mum has been away, passed over for a year and a half, it's very little time on the other side." (' Right. '). " And, so your mum's sister, seems to be petite."

(I'm not sure why I didn't tell Claudette at this time, that my mum didn't have a sister. My dad did, two or three.).

"She says, ' Just a minute. I'll go get her. '. I'll let her go off ... it's like 'B'... 'Beat'... I feel it was a nickname, that she had this auntie of yours. It wasn't her full name. But, you would have... um... Yorkshire... did anybody come from Yorkshire county?"

(' Could have. '). " She's telling me ' Yorkshire County '... and then, who went to Liverpool? Worked in the coal mines. Who would have worked... do you have any idea? (' No. I didn't know any of them. '). " Okay. Well, this is information you can verify."

"Anyways... yes... um.. was your mum in her eighties, when she passed?"

(' Ninety-three. '). "Okay, did she have an affliction at eighty-something?" (' She had a number of afflictions over the years. '). " In the eighties, I'm talking about eighty... at eighty, it shifted her. In other words, I'm being told that at eighty there was an affliction that weakened her. And, she couldn't do as much as she wanted to, because your mother was very... go, go, go." (' Definitely. '). " I want my legs.. I want everything." (' Yes. '). " At eighty, she lost that mobility. She was very upset about that. She became very bitter about that. Difficult in some ways because of it. I hear her say ' look at me now. I can dance, I can...(Claudette laughing) Here's a woman that enjoyed life." ('Oh yes. She was a riot. '). " Truly enjoyed life... singing and dancing, whatever." ('Absolutely. '). " And, participating... a participant in life. And, she comes in with this love... I feel this great love here, that is being generated from her, and her excitement... jois vivre... and that sort of thing. And, I hear her say, ' you're a poor specimen for... for participation,' (Laughing.) she says, ' you got to enjoy life more.' So, she wants you to enjoy life. So, she's looking at you and she says you're a poor imitation of jois vivre. She says you have to get out there... you're young... enjoy... before it's too late. (Both laughing). So, she's encouraging you to be motivated to enjoy life, do you understand, please?" (' Yes. ') " Giggle, and laugh, and so on. Because she says you really do have a good sense of humor, you just have to use it. She says the more that you allow that bubbly self that you really are... because there was a real bonding between the two of you."

(' Definitely. Yes '). "There's a strong bond here, like I can feel so much love here for you, and it's like you were her boy. I know you were her son... but I mean really her boy." (' Yes. '). "You could do no wrong. She was saddened that things didn't work out for you with your marriage, but at the same time... it was all her fault not yours, of course." (' Claudette laughing.'). (Me. ' Right, laughing.'). "But... she just counted a lot on you... getting things done, and so on and so forth. And now, the thing that she wants the most for you is to be happy, and enjoy life, no matter what, enjoy life. Giggle, laugh, see the humor in yourself, and don't allow yourself to be dragged down." (' Right. ').

"She says, ' I've just been here it feels like seconds, it's still very new '. And so, she's doing the rounds, getting to see and visit everybody, etc. And then she says ' I'm going to '... *what's she say*... ' we can choose in which area we want to be in.' She says, ' I'm still considering. Still looking. I want to know how this all works.'

(' That would be her. '). "Let me first examine things and see how it works before I decide, sort of thing."

"Would you understand Herbert, ... Hubert.... the first, middle or last name? Albert? (' My middle name is Albert, after an uncle of mine. '). Is your uncle in spirit? (' Yes. All my aunts and uncles have passed. '). The ...' bert' is in there, I'm trying to find out... we don't always get it clearly, so I'm asking her, 'are we talking about Albert, or... *yes, okay*...no it's Albert. Just to gain evidence that it is her, do you understand, please? (' Yes, okay.'). And, did she ever call you Albert at some time? (' No. '). Who called you Albert, please? ('Nobody.'). Nobody ever called you that? ('No.').

(Quietly. *So why are you telling me this?*) Then it would have to be...Albert...Is Albert related to her, please?" (' I don't think so. I think it was my dad's side.')

Claudette: "Okay. Was your dad... I still have your dad here. (Laughing). Okay. Did your dad work with his hands? ('Yes.'). Yes, thank you... umm... and he's giving me this crooked smile. (Laughing). And, he's looking at your mother, and he's giving her the look...(Laughing.)... they're looking at each other...comedy sort of thing... not saying anything, just looking. Questions, please, before we run out of time."

Mike: "The only ... um... I'm just wondering about a couple of other people, maybe. Dick and Marilyn were good friends of mine, and if my son John is around?" ('Oh, the little boy...'). "Yes, the little boy that was..."

Claudette: "And, have you been listening to music...hearing music in your head, please? (' Oh, yes. All the time.'). Every time you hear that music in your head, it's your son John. And, he's around you. And ask, ' Is that you John? Are you around me? And, wait. Wait. Get to know what a yes and a no is. ('Okay.'). So, you can say, ' Is that you, John? ' and ' I'm hearing the music, is that you? Let me feel you. Let me sense you.'. Alright? And then, wait to feel a response. Don't get up here. Sense. Always feel sense to know. ('Okay.'). Then, when it's John, you'll feel expanded or you'll feel love. If it's no then... sort of thing. Because your own imagination...you're own mind plugs in kind of thing. You need to learn to know the difference when it's your mind, versus spirit trying to communicate with you.

So, John is here to look you up, and help you on that sense of humor of yours. I hear... I keep hearing all of them at the same time say, ' don't give up on yourself ' Alright? ('Yes.'). Because there's a part of you as... as much bravado as you have... there's a part of you that at times gives up, do you understand? (' Yes. Well, I get frustrated. '). Yes, and I hear, ' don't give up on yourself.' When you get frustrated, take a nice deep breathe, go for a walk,...' all is well...all is well... I'm one with God, I'm one with Source'... whatever you call it."

"You're also a nature buff. ('Yep.'). You love nature. And I see you in a park or nature, and it just revives you... ('Absolutely. It does.')... and I hear, ' just take nature walks'. Even if you start belonging to the trail club, you know the ones that have walking trails, or whatever. It's a good way of meeting people, of being part of a group, that kind of thing. Any other questions?"

Mike: "Marilyn?" (' The couple... '). "Dick and Marilyn?"

Claudette: "They have their own thing. They're doing their own thing, now. Just know that once you cross over to spirit, you don't have to be with the same husband and wife.('No, no I know.'). They are very much into healing. Marilyn is into greeting people who cross over traumatized. (' Oh, okay.'). She's working in greeting... you know people that cross over due to elements... like storms, ...earthquakes... (' tornadoes ')... yes, that kind of thing... you know one minute they're here the next they're on the other side, but it's all fast and confusing.... and Dick is also involved more with the youth... ah... because there has been a lot of suicides with youth, kind of thing, and he seems to be into the youth kind of environment... helping out. ('Okay'.) So, they're working as helpers from the other side."

"And, who would have crossed over in a car accident?... *yes, thank you*... car accident, crash... I get car crash... major crash. And, I feel a fellow that didn't die immediately, but would have been real quick afterwards... (Pause. I'm thinking.). Do you understand a Peter? (' I've got a brother, Peter.). He's not in spirit is he? ('No.').

No... (Quietly)...okay is this associated with Peter. ('I have a very good friend Peter, but I haven't seen him in a number of years, so I don't know...'). I just... um... I feel somebody that would have crossed over, and I get the name 'Peter'. So, this is not your brother Peter, he's here. So, this is a Peter that is on the other side, not associated to your brother. It is a gentleman that crossed over by the name of Peter, and again, I get this whole thing about... just put Peter on the shelf, and you wait until he brings whoever... so that you can pass on the message that he did cross over. ('Okay.'). There's always this concern, people that die quickly, that they didn't make it over, and this fellow, Peter... and somehow you know his family, or... at some point you are going to cross paths with somebody... and then... ah hah. ('Okay, I'll remember that'.). And, somebody will say, ' I wonder if he made it?'. Then, you can say... 'ah, I know he did'. (Claudette ' yes, I got goose bumps on that'.). So, you're the message bearer on that. So, Peter's okay. Made it.

Again, it's his fault. Good. Question?"

Mike: "Um... one more... my wife's daughter, Lisa. She's been there for five or six years... ('In spirit?')... in spirit for five or six years, yes."

Claudette: "Was she very ill for a period of time? ('Yes. She had lung cancer'). Okay, because when I get this...erpp...kind of vomiting... it's cancer."

Mike: "Actually, my wife came to see you after it happened, just because she was very upset about the whole thing, and umm... so, I was just wondering how she's doing."

Claudette: "She's really doing well. Because I see...I see a young lady that's smiling, and doing really well. Like to me, she's got this beautiful energy around her... she's got this beautiful white, lavender energy around her, which to me is a very good progressive soul, doing really well." ('Oh, that's good.').

"Working with babies... ('Oh, really.')... *yes, thank you*...and so, she's assisting in that environment......she loves babies... ('Good. I'll pass that on to her mom. She'll like that'). She's advanced... she's doing much better. She's adjusted to being on the other side. And, you know guys, five, six years is like five or six minutes...(' Yes, I know that...')... there's no time... ('There's no...I know, I realize that.')...As I see her... I see her just oozing this beautiful energy, right? And, ah... it was the way that she chose to cross over. It was to help her soul progression... to do it on the earth plane, then she doesn't have to do it on the other side. So, these were all things that mom had to also experience in her journey." ('Yes.').

"So, Lisa is really doing well... that's how she says it, ' I'm really doing well... and I'm looking after the babies.' ('That sounds just like her.'). Yes, (Laughing)... she's got this excitement... yes... and she says 'thank you...thank you for being there for me'... and she says 'I know the toll it took on mom, and you, and thank you for being there for me... you didn't have to.' She's appreciative for that. She's happy that she has the opportunity to express her gratitude, what a difference you made in her life as well, when she needed a father... when she needed somebody, a male figure. And she says ' You know what? Nobody's perfect...and that's okay... you all did what you could at the time... and um... yes...just tell mom to stop mourning me, and just to enjoy life. ('Yes.'). That she's doing great. She's working with the angels. ('Oh good.'). And, she comes to visit her mom... 2:30, 3:00 o'clock in the morning. If mom wakes up, that's fine... but she comes to visit, to say hello and check in on her...so, if mom can just say, 'Is that you, Lisa?', when she wakes up... and um... then they can start communicating, or feeling each other, do you understand, please?" ('Yes'.). " Spirit is a tenable energy, just like you and I, just don't have the physical."

"And.. Godfrey...who is Godfrey? Do you know a Godfrey? Geez, these names... are coming... (Me laughing. 'I don't know.'). Godfrey. Who are you, please?

Ah...' I am a guide.' ('Oh.'). He's a guide. ('Good.'). I feel a new guide, and somebody to just kind of get you going."

Mike: "Because I had Arthur, and then I had Jack. And Jack should have left by now, I think."

Claudette: "So, we've got a Godfrey. Godfrey. You know the name, right? ('Yes.'). I feel that Godfrey's here for your spiritual development... as in your sense of feeling, linking in for your higher guidance...stuff like that. ('Oh, good.'). So, he's here to move you forward, and he says 'you need discipline, and you need commitment.' That's the only way you're going to move forward. ('Okay.'). And, dedication too, as well as being able to deal with this world, etc."

"And, I also feel that when you do your meditation, you need to call in... your, what I call the Alchemist guide... it's a guide which is the *chemist*. His and her responsibility is to shift your frequency. So, what happens is they come in, and you want to say, ' I call upon my Alchemist guide, to shift and change my frequency. Help me move to a higher frequency. So, please come closer, closer, closer still. Let me feel you. Let me sense you.'"

"Once you feel that presence with you, just say, ' I'm open now to shift.' Then, we go to the next step. There will be like different steps and then will bring you back. Then, say ' I offer myself to the shift and change. If I do lose my consciousness, bring me back within 20 minutes,'... or whatever. That's very important. ('Okay.'). So, that will help you in shifting your frequency. Again, as you do the *GAPP*, that will help you... I didn't get the name of your Alchemist, you'll have to ask. You need to have an identity for each of your guides. So that at least you say ' is this you Godfrey?... is this you Arthur?'. ('Okay.'). That way you know who you're working with. That's another thing... that's another premise that we have to have... is that you need to know who you're working with, because anybody can come near you, and you make an assumption; and, that's not a good thing. We're not to make assumptions, or judgments, or whatever. It demonstrates our discipline. It's just like in your physical world, you wouldn't just invite anybody in.

You'd know who you're inviting in... ('Right.')...same with spirit, guides or otherwise. People feel vibration, and they immediately assume it's a guide. Well, it may not be. It could be a loved one visiting, it could be an entity, who knows. Does that help?"

(' Yes, definitely, yes.').

"So, I want to say Mike, life is changing, and it's continuing. You're still on that... um...changing, shifting, for the next two years, anyways... do you understand? And, as you continue on, just know that you're heading for a brighter, more clear, and astute kind of future spiritually...and I feel that the physical world will all take care of itself. Because as you work on that, that spirituality of yours...when you do the *GAPP* every day, it just shifts your energy, therefore it's the *Law of Attraction,* see? You want to have the funds, and the ability and the freedom to do all the stuff that you need to do. No one is meant to be poor. ('No.'). It's just we choose to. It's just the effort, it's like at this point you need to make the effort, and put closure on things, and say ' I'm freeing myself for my future.' Be open. Keep having an open mind, and an open heart, and things will all fall into place. And at that, we'll say ' God bless, and thank you."

Mike: "Thank you. "

So, it's been three years since my last session with Claudette, and I was interested to see who might come through, or what comments she may have for me.

Since that last session, I have left the brokerage business, and am now working as a Security Officer at a local hospital. It's quite a change from my previous job, but I like what I'm doing. The guys I work with are a lot younger than me, but are good guys and I get along with them fine. Once I leave work it's forgotten. There's no worrying at night about what the next day is going to bring, which was sometimes the case in the market. And with a steady 40 hour week and paycheck plus sometimes overtime and holiday pay, I'm doing a lot better.

Okay, right off the bat when Claudette mentioned the name ' Paul ', I thought of my childhood friend. It's like just thinking of him gave her confirmation that that's who it was. Once again I got that tingling sensation in my body, acknowledging that spirit was present. We were good friends though, but not what you would call best friends. We went to the same high school, and I used to get a ride to school with him and his father sometimes. I don't remember anything about marbles. I was 14 at the time, past marbles. But maybe there is a hidden meaning there that I didn't get. We were in the same class for three years, then my family moved out west. It was when I went back for a visit a year or two later that I heard what happened to him. My understanding is that this was his first dating experience, and he was deeply and emotionally involved. After some time the girlfriend broke it off. I believe Paul may have had a fragile psyche, and the rejection was too much for him. There's confirmation when Claudette gets a throat and chest condition, verifying the hanging. He had a large family, lots of brothers and sisters. Someone found him in the basement one day where he had hung himself. I'm not sure if I will ever run into any of his family, but if I do I will pass along the message that it was no one's fault.

It was good to hear from my father again. I appreciate his comments, and though we did butt heads at times, I never doubted that he loved me.

I didn't get the person Judy coming through until a long time afterwards. I had a client named Judy. (Apart from trading, I also had a few clients that I did some transactions for.) Judy was a friend, though not a close one to me. She was a closer friend to Verine. They went to school together. She's the only Judy I could think of. She passed after a battle with cancer. Maybe because I didn't acknowledge her right away, she gave up, and didn't try re-communicating. As I've said, sometimes you don't connect right away in a sitting until later.

I do believe I need coaching, as I don't seem to be progressing that much on my own. Right now I'm working nights, and I don't sleep that well during the day, so weekends is when I try to catch up with my rest, which doesn't leave me a lot of time for other things.

I am trying to focus more on the heart and less from the mind when I'm meditating. I get a very strong vibration in my brow area (brow or sixth chakra) as soon as I start meditating. I can easily bring it on at will, just by briefly thinking of it, at any time. I have to concentrate more on the other chakras (Root/Base, Sacral, Solar Plexus, Heart, Throat, Brow, Crown.) to feel a sensation.

We have a number of spirit guides that are there to help us at any time for anything, BUT... we have to ask. They respect our free will, and will not intervene, as much as I'm sure they'd like to, without a request from us.

We have Joy guides, Healing or Doctor guides, Animal or Totem guides, Protector guides, and Teacher guides. These are a few of the main ones, but there are actually many more.

Some guides stay with us all the way through our stay in physical, while others come and go according to the assistance or teachings we need at a particular moment. So, I had Arthur for a couple of years, then Jack, and now Godfrey. John, my son is acting as a Joy guide for me. My friend Kim, has said that he is not a guide but someone who is willing to help whenever I need it, which is appreciated.

Once again there is the mention of marriage in the next few years. As I've gotten older, I have to say I don't have a real positive outlook on the institution of marriage, especially going by the divorce rate. That's not to say I wouldn't do it again if the right person comes along, and it's important to them. At my age, there's a good chance it would last. Ha Ha. It would be nice to have someone, and to compliment each other. I do appreciate my independence, but it would be nice to have someone with similar interests to share with.

I never made a connection to a woman with the letter B, or with a Marge...Margaret. I may have to dig further into my English relatives.*

(* Very much later I realized that I did know a Marge from when I worked at the Billy Bishop Legion. She wasn't a relative but a good friend with my mother, and always acted like sort of an aunt figure to me. I wonder if that might have been her.)

My mother definitely enjoyed life. She was the life of the party at any age. She said what she thought, even more so as she got older, and would get everyone laughing in no time. If she got on a bus, by the time she got off, she'd know half the people and what they were up to. I don't see myself as someone who doesn't enjoy life, but I guess compared to her, I am a poor specimen. There's no doubt that there was a strong bond between the two of us.

She was a wonderful artist, which she didn't really get to until later in life, when everyone had moved out. So she was very excited when I started dabbling in it myself. She'd pick out a picture and we would both paint it, and then compare them. She'd win.

Because there is no time on the other side, I can see her being there quite a while, getting around and visiting with so many friends. She loved babies and children, and was a nanny, before the war started, so I can see her getting into something like that over there.

I do seem to have music playing in my head almost all the time, and I do love nature. It must go back to when I was younger. Dad would insist quite often on a Sunday that the family go for a walk together in the parks or forests. As I got into my teens, I would rather hang out with my friends. No way. Dad made me go along with the rest of the family. Butting heads again. But once I got there it was always good. Both my parents were great walkers. I think that was why mom made it as long as she did.

It was wonderful to hear about my friends Dick and Marilyn. They did a lot of good work for others when they were here, and it's no surprise that they're continuing that on the other side.

I'll have to wait for someone to ask me about this Peter person.

It was also good to hear from Lisa and that beautiful energy she was giving off.

So once again this was the way she chose to pass. This was something that she chose to experience for her soul progression, and also something that her mom had to experience and get through likewise.

I will call on the *Alchemist* guide to help me shift my frequency when I do my meditations. The first thing I do when I begin a meditation is surround myself with ' Divine or White Light ', as a protection against any negativity or bad vibrations that may try to creep in. I'm not sure, but there could be negative entities that may try to affect your energy. Better safe than sorry.

A couple of things that Claudette briefly touched on were *earth shifts* and *other dimensions.* There definitely is something going on with our planet. Mother Earth is a living entity, and it's almost like she's fighting back to survive what we are putting her through...more and more cataclysmic events, like hurricanes, tornadoes, flooding, horrendous forests fires, the ice caps melting, etc., to wake us up. I have also been reading about a *spiritual awakening/ spiritual shift* that has begun according to many visionaries/ seers.

As for other dimensions, it's a subject of which volumes have been written. There's the *spiritual* dimension, and those who believe that there are any number of dimensions and universes. I'm going to leave it at that, because it's too broad a topic for a quick thought on my part. I will say that I personally believe that there is much more out there.

So again, I was very pleased with the reading. Those who came through, interesting things to contemplate, and more insights for me to start working on.

My grandfather on my mother's side as a young man. (Boer War) This is the uniform I believe Claudette saw. It doesn't go down far enough to show the leggings, but I have seen a picture with the full view, I just couldn't find it.

*My Mother, Grandfather and Uncle George. I
believe this is in Quebec City, when my grandfather
became ill and the family returned to England.*

My Mother, Nanny, sister Sue, and myself. Bayside, New York.

Dad, with cowboy hat that Claudette saw. (In Fourth Session.)

1942. Mom and some friends from her school days.

Marriage of Mom and Dad. Lots of aunts, uncles, grandparents and cousins. Sometime near the start of the war, and dad would be shipping out for North Africa at some point. Mom drove supply trucks in England and knew more about engines than I ever did.

Mom 1989. She'd be 73. She was a hoot.

*My good friends Dick & Marilyn. Best of the best. Still
bantering about why Dick passed before her.*

*Toby. 'I'm too busy. I'm too busy.' Cute little guy, but
had his own feistiness and personality. Very smart.*

FOURTH SESSION

Sept. 20, 2013 Session with Claudette.

Claudette: "Breathe. Take a nice deep breathe. We're going to make that ...awww... sound, just to release and detach from the physical world so that we can move into a good sacred space. So, breathe in...awww...and with that intent, I detach, detach, detach. Again, breathe in...awww...good. Better. Another one, please...breathe in... awww... Release all the stress of getting here, preparing, and the world. Last one... deep breathe...awww. Good one."

"Okay. I'm just going to say a prayer. Just relax. Open your mind, open your heart. As I start with prayer. ' Infinite Spirit, Divine Mother God, we ask for a blessing on this sitting. We ask for the highest and the best clarity of mind, direction and understanding.'. Okay, Mike... it is Mike, right? ('Yes.') Mike, as I was saying the prayer, I just began to see the energies form, and then open up, and then this beautiful little elder lady, I would say, now to me she looks like a grandmother. And, she's petite, and she comes in, a little plumpish, short... didn't like to be called short, she had a thing about her height. And, she comes in with such loving vibration, one that would have been nurtured through food, which was part of their time, but I feel also that you were very special to her, please. Do you have a grandmother in spirit, that you could do no wrong? ('Yes.') And, she was very nurturing. ('Yes.') And you know, you were like her Mikey, kind of... come here... and... aww don't worry about that...always soothing, comforting, and looking after you. Where you know, there was troubled times in your life, and she was that burst of love that you would need when you felt like nothing in this world worked for you. And, I also feel that there's a gentleman that would have been in the forces, please... *yes, thank you.* Was this your grandfather, please?"

Mike: "I had a lot of my family in the forces."

Claudette: "Okay, I want a gentleman that was in the army. This one was in the army."

Mike: "Yes, they all were."

Claudette: "Oh, they all were. Okay, do you have...this gentleman presents himself in uniform, but he also has...I feel that he had like a level... like a Captain, Sergeant, or something...he was in charge. He holds the bugle with his hand, as well. So, I feel that he's coming in... and I feel that there's the letter 'J'... like James, or Jack... the letter 'J.'"

Mike: "Okay. I didn't.. I didn't...all my relatives were in Britain, so I didn't know most of them."

Claudette: "Alright, so let me just get the information from him. I identify him as an uncle... standing very upright, and he had the cap... like he would be... and he has some markings... I'm not knowledgeable enough in that... but I feel that he would have been an officer...*thank you*...he gives me the look like 'ignorant woman here, who doesn't have that information. (Claudette laughing) Not as in a negative word, but not educated enough. ('Ha Ha'.) We're not supposed to complain about the messenger. (Laughing.)."

Mike: "Is this world War II, maybe?"

Claudette: "I feel more World War II...*yes, thank you*...and, he's stands very upright, very in charge, very much so, and as he holds the bugle, he says ' I brought you the bugle... the call has been made for you. It's time... it's time to make the steps... it's time to move forward'. I also feel that you Mike, that you are very Spiritual. That there's a very strong Spiritual aspect to you that needs to be evolved, and developed. You need to move on with it. ('Okay') And, I feel that it's in your blood... and grandmother is saying, ' yes, it's part of who you are and you need to accept that'. She came with love, to be recognized, to bring the love, and she also loved flowers...a beautiful garden, flowers...I'm seeing all kinds of different colors of flowers. If it was up to her, she would have had a whole field of flowers that would bloom at different times, different seasons."

"I also feel though, that you are at that point in your life where things are shifting, changing, and moving, you need to make decisions, do you understand? ('Yes') You need to decide, ' I'm going with this, or not '. And, I feel it's that ' yes, no... but, but, but 'kind of thing, that self doubt that filters in. I want to say, that you need to follow that gut feeling. These wonderful souls...*oh yes, thank you...* I see a dog with you as well, please, and I want to say a medium sized dog, longish hair, fair haired, or brownish color kind of thing. Do you have a dog in spirit, please? (' Yes, I have a few. ') Yes, this is more...more like a border collie, or something like that. ('Okay') I feel that this dog would have been a mixed breed. ('Yes, he was'). He comes again to be recognized. I feel that he was a great partner to you, because this one dog...there was a special connection with him.. so he's here with you as well. ('Okay') He says I never left you. And there's also an aspect of you that's a very sensitive individual. Sometimes you see it as a curse. This is not a curse, it's an asset, because of your journey on earth. You need that intuition. You need to understand."

"Have you been back to England, please? ('No.') You need to go to England. You need to see that there are many people that are male in the spiritual environment. You need to see it, because there's not many here in Canada. You need to investigate that, you need to research it, and see how you can develop yourself. You gotta make the steps, do you understand?" ('Yes.')

"I also feel that...*yes, thank you...*that in your physical world, there's been many challenges. And, basically a relationship with life which has affected your lifelong relationships. It's been a yes and no, yes and no, kind of thing. And, I feel that you have settled in to a... how do I say... a little bit of a blasé kind of ... oh well, whatever...and you have to get rid of that one. So, it's about trusting, and trusting yourself again. It's like you meet people...are you presently married? ('No.') Okay, so, I feel that it's like, ' I meet a potential partner', and you test the waters, if you like, and, 'naw, that doesn't feel right', it's because you're trying to make it work. When it is the right partner, you don't need to make it work, it's a happening.

('Okay.') And, I feel that that is there for you...as we say the expression 'it's in the cards' for you, do you understand? ('Yes.') It's a matter of starting to trust, trust your heart, because you're a very...you love deeply, that's the thing. And, it's the attitude, 'well, I don't want to just love anybody, it's got to be worthy of my love', kind of thing, and I don't mean that in a negative way. But, you know what, it's about allowing that radiation of love to leave your heart, to draw the right person to you. ('Okay.') It's not about looking, it's about drawing the person. It's all about energy, and magnetizing the right person for a partnership, if you like, as in romance, lifelong type of partner, but also in everything else in your life. You're at that point where your...it's like you move through the veil."

"How old are you now? ('Sixty-six.') So, at sixty-five, that's when life changed for you, right? Sixty-four, was about letting go...sixty-four to sixty-five... 'okay, I don't need this, I can let it go'. Once I reached sixty-five, it was about attaining... ' I have to adjust to my new life, or my new vibration'. You know you've waited all your life to do what you want to. And, it's time...like the bugle again... sound it... the call has been made. And, I see a lot of angels around you. Do you believe in angels? (' Oh definitely, yes. ') So, I want to say from sixty-five to seventy-one is about establishing or building the kind of life that is right for you, not right for this one or that one, you know...because you are also very responsible person, so you wouldn't release things easily. You want to...it's about the trust factor here as well, because it feels like a trust... a trust... oh... 'I've been hurt from it', and it's about ' Okay, that's passé. I'm a different person today. I'm more confident. I'm more ready for a dedication of my time', do you see? ('Sure.') Because through the work environment, through the process of your life, you wanted and worked, but you were also needing to provide...the money, and this and that...the pressures and so on, and not dedicating enough time too. Whereas now you can dedicate the time. And so, in your wisdom, you have acquired the knowledge that 'You know what, money's not everything. I need it to establish what I want to, but it's not everything. I need a balance of things.' I feel that you're heading for that."

"You said your sixty-six, so sixty-five to sixty-six was about following through the decisions that you have made. Making the change, not just ' Oh, I think it is...' But actually taking the steps, and you have taken three major steps, thus far. Are you still working, please? ('Yes.') Yes, so one of the steps is 'do I still want to continue working.'"

Mike: "I know the answer to that, ha ha."

Claudette: "Right. And again, it's about 'can I afford to or not.'(Laughing). ('Yes, exactly.') But, there's a difference with working, and working on a full time basis, working on a part time. You're not the type of person to just sit around twiddling your thumbs. You're not that kind of person. So, what you have to do is shift and change your attention to the areas that are important to you. There are certain personalities that never want to stop working. It doesn't mean...the difference is that we come to a point where we say 'I'm not a slave to it.' 'I can choose.' There's a difference here. ('Right.') So, this is where you're at, where you can learn to choose the time, choose the place, choose the things, does that make sense to you?"('Yes. Yes.').

"Would you understand a John, or Johnny, please in spirit? Do you have a young...a young man...um."

Mike: "John, my son."

Claudette: "Yes. Son, yes...I was just about to say 'do you have a son in spirit?'. *Yes, thank you... Yes, thank you.*

Just came forward, and he says ' you haven't changed.' (Both laughing) But he comes with a...*yes John*...he comes with a...(Quietly) what does he say...'he's a hard... nut to crack' he says. (Both laughing) Would you understand that, please?'

Mike: "Well, you know, my son was... never...he was never...um...never actually born."

Claudette: "He was stillborn, miscarried."

Mike: "He was...aborted...it was a long time ago and..."

Claudette: "Okay, yes. So, he must have come through before, right? ('He has, yes.') So, John here is saying 'he's a hard nut to crack', and he says 'but I've been working on him.' (' Oh, okay.') He's here with you, but he also comes interestingly enough...he comes with a horse, please. Do you like horses, or been around horses?"

Mike: "I mean I've ridden horses, and things like that, but I..."

Claudette: "He comes with a horse, and again it's part of who you are. ('Oh.') So, it's just to show that...the horse would indicate it's part of your past, it's part of who you've been, etc, etc. ('Okay'.) He's coming around and he says ' well, dad, I keep trying to move you forward, and change your mind about certain things, but you're resistant', he says. John here says ' I have the patience of Job.' ('That's good'.) (Both laughing). He obviously...he's using expressions that you would understand. ('Yes.') He comes with such great love, and such joy, and respect, and there's a strong connection here between the two of you, even though he didn't breathe, or didn't live a life on earth, he's definitely been with you as if he was on earth. ('Yes, I agree.'). That close, right?

('Yes.') And he says, 'you know what, it's time we get back on the horse, and that we go to the country, and we start...' See nature is your medicine, do you understand, please? ('Yes, definitely.') You need to get out there, when you need to think, to think things out, whether it's a horse, whether it's a walk, whether it's a car, whether it's a mustang...

(Claudette laughing)... car, mustang...did you have a mustang at one time?"

Mike: "I didn't, but I almost bought one about six months ago. I was that close to buying it, but then I didn't at the last minute."

Claudette: "Well, there you go, see? Again, he knows, because I'm seeing a mustang. Just to show that he's aware of this, because again, it was right there with him. But he says, you know that you need to just take the quiet and go and sort things out. You're not one that listens well. (Claudette laughing) And, I don't mean that derogatory, I just mean that when people are full of advice, you say 'thank you' and you just kind of ...(shrug)...that sort of thing. So, what I want to say to you, is sometimes as you do your *GAPP*, or you talk to the Divine or whatever... the Divine may send you Ambassadors, and people that don't even know what they're talking about, but there will be something in what they say that answers your question, do you understand, please?"

Mike: "Yes, I actually know that they are trying to get through to me, but I'm not paying attention, I guess to what's coming my way...or I'm not getting it... or something..."

Claudette: "Okay."

Mike: "Like, I'm trying...I'm communicating with them, and I'm sure their coming back...communicating back to me, but I'm not quite...tuned in to it, or whatever."

Claudette: "Okay. There's a difference, you see. As you're expressing, talking, and they're responding...you don't have to hear it the way I do or see it, but it can become that. So, if they can't reach you this way, what they do is they use a person that's going to be on your path, that has no clue what it's all about, ...will say something out of turn or out of whatever...and you say ' Ah ha, there's my sign '. So, you have to start watching the signs, the words, the music. Sometimes you put on the radio, and you say ' oh, there's that song I was thinking about '."(' Yes.')

"Or different things like that...or in the dreams, see? So, when you're more at peace. (' I have a lot of dreams.') The dreams can be...so, you have to start journaling. The dreams can be the answer to the questions...or some direction...or showing you the way, because it's time, and I feel that the time that I'm talking about *'it's the time'*, it's about merging and blending your spiritual self, the unit self, the physical self, and becoming all your full potential. You've proven yourself on the physical, material world...it's time now to work on your spiritual self. That's where you're at...you've moved into that part of your life, because you're here for the long term, you know. ('Okay'.) So take care of yourself. We want quality life here, we don't want it kind of agghhh...You know the aches and pains, whatever. Have you noticed as you got older, the aches and pains are faster than they used to be? (Claudette Laughing). ('Yes.') So, it's just a matter of having a balance in your life. You need to find a balance."

"Now, I see you dancing please. Do you enjoy dancing, or you don't like dancing?"

Mike: "I....I mean I like dancing, yes, but I don't really do it a lot. (Me laughing)."

Claudette: "No, no...it's very difficult to go to a place to do dancing now. ('Yes. But...I like to dance') Okay, because I see that...that swaying, that...rhythm, and

I actually see you dancing. So, may I recommend that you take dancing lessons, so that you can meet people that are interested in that. It doesn't matter whether it's ballroom dancing, or whatever, but what draws you...be it country dancing, ballroom, it doesn't matter. Something to get you into a balance. ('Okay'.) It's either that or singing. Which one are you going to take?"

Mike: "I like to sing too."

Claudette: "Oh, nooo... (Laughing) So, then we have a choir. Again, that's you're creative side, expression. You see when you sing, you move into a whole different world. Same with your dancing. When you used to dance, way back when, you would move into a different world, you see? You became a different person. It's the same with your singing. So that's the creative side that needs to be expressed. You need to do something creative, so it's either taking dancing lessons, joining a choir, or art, do you understand? ('I do art too.') Oh, okay, so there you go. You can develop that , work with that, because you see with the art, you can design something that can help people to meditate as well. Do you do watercolors, or oils? ('I do both.') Both. Okay. I feel that you can create the art, where it can be used as a domain for, or a media for people to move into an altered state."

(' Okay.')

"So, think about that, and create that, because there's a lot of satisfaction, and rewards there for you as well. So, you're moving into the physical, into more of the creative, and still getting revenue from it. And, I hear you can also write?"

Mike: "Um, I have done a little bit of writing, but... and it's mostly to do with this. You know, like our...sort of our sessions...and what it meant to me, and..."

Claudette: "The journaling. So, I feel that you can also...as you develop...you could be writing a book, a channeled book. It's just about sitting down, and just letting yourself write whatever comes through. Basically, what that means is that...and it takes time to actually get whatever the book is, kind of thing. The first step is to sit with pen and paper and just write your thoughts...just write, write, write, write... until eventually, then you know that you're working with...I feel that you have a guide here that can help you to be the author, and work with you on that as well. ('Okay'.) And, I feel that the book can be a variety of things... it can be a self help book, it can be a novel...it can be different types of things. You've got that creative juice in you that you need to express. And, this is it. Sixty-five to seventy-one is all about your creative self, and evolving your spiritual self to be a stronger partner with your physical self. This is it, now. Once you reach seventy-one, it's like ... .'aahh well...I can't be bothered, to old...do this, do that...' that kind of thing. So, now's the time to do it." ('Okay.')

"And, I feel that you can travel to England, you can go to the *Arthur Findlay* College. You can take courses there, just to get to know different people, and how everyone... you'll meet the right stimulus there to get you going. It's about being on the journey and exploring. You need to look at things as an exploration. Look at all the creative things that you can do, and start getting involved in this again. And, I feel that we move from full time physical work or material work, to part time, and part time spiritual, so we have a blend of both, do you understand?" ('Okay.')

"This is the time. Do your part time work, because you like to get out and do your...you can't just let it go...it's just not one of those things. And, you're the type of person that will always want to do the material work anyhow, it doesn't matter what it is. There's a lot of...I want to say you're a *jack of all trades* type of thing, you can do many things, right? ('Yes.') So, it's not just one thing, you're really... there's many things you can put your fingers in. Now, let's get to your questions before we run out of time."

Mike: "I guess ... I guess you kind of answered the one I had."

Claudette: "What was that?"

Mike: "Well, what's in store in the near future, and the next couple of years."

Claudette: "Okay, for the next couple of...let's address that again. So, let's see if we can get a little more on that. Sixty-six right now. Did you just turn sixty-six, please? ('Six months ago.') Okay, so you're moving into...you're half way into your sixty-seventh...the reason I say that is there's three and a half years basically to get on with it...now I want you to know that...are you self employed, please? ('No.') No. You're working for somebody, right? ('Yes.') Are you able to move into a part time kind of work environment?"

Mike: "I can, yes. In truth, I rather just be totally retired. ('Right.') But, I can't really afford it right now. But, I can do part time."

Claudette: "So, you can ease into it? ('Right.') What I hear is, to move into part time, which then affords you more time to explore that spiritual aspect. Even though you want to be full time retired, let's move first part time, so that you can explore... you still have the revenue coming in, a little bit of security, you've got your CPP (Canada Pension Plan) and everything... ('Yes.') so just to kind of ease into it. And, I feel that the next tier is about that. And so, there's been a draw....um...this has been stirring within you for the last two to three years. ('Yes.') Right. Usually spirit will start two years ahead of time, and get things stirring so that there's that strong desire...'okay, I know my time is up here, I need to move on'. You'd be wise and do it on a bridge kind of thing. You've already got your six months in, possibly another six months to a year. I want to say about a year. Next year about this time you're ready, you're ready to let go, and you will trust and believe that your art work can bring the revenue, do you understand, please? ('Yes, okay.')"

"I'm not asking you to play on the band, or go and sing in a band, but your art work is going to bring in revenue. What we want to do, is have your special time, or your time off, like holidays or whatever, where you can travel in an area where you can learn more about what we're talking about...your spiritual development, and go places where you meet people from all over the world...that there are men from all over the world that are like you. You need to know that there are guys in this. Going back to England where your roots are...you can also have some closure on that. So, take a holiday. Check in at the *Arthur Findlay College,* which is a mediumistic college, and you can look at what time of year that there are courses there that you would like to take. They also have *'spirit art'*...all kinds of wonderful things there... some wonderful tutors. But, asked to be guided. And while you're there, then you spend your time there...and then you spend another week, you know traveling in the areas that are home...the roots of your family. ('Sure.') And, I feel that as you do that...you learn, and see, and meet so many different types of people...and it fulfills you. Because Canada is big, but there is not a lot of opportunities for that growth, etc...depending where you are, where you live."

" Where do you live, please? ('I live in Vancouver') Okay. But even there...in our area of B.C., there isn't that many...there are a lot of psychics, a lot of mediums...but very few that are that very strong, you know that kind of thing... and no offense to anybody. But you know...I don't know everybody that's here ('I understand')...I'm just saying it's good to go also to...and one of the spots is either *Lily Dale* in New York, ("I know of Lily Dale.) or the *Arthur Findlay College* in England. And, they now have Centres, *Arthur Findlay Centres,* they are expanding...and various places, but those are the hubs that have the expertise. Because there are a lot of people out in the world, that call themselves such and such...so, it's up to you, what you are drawn to, but again, my message that I hear for you, is that it's time for you now to evolve that and move forward. So, we move part time work into part time spiritual investment, or exploration, and development."

"Art is very important to you. You just have the knack, you have the touch, do you understand? ('Okay.') I'd love to see you develop...ah... 'spirit portraits', spirit art. And so, there's the *auragraphs* that you can do with spirit...spirit just takes over, and it's always beautiful. Then there's also 'spirit portraits' kind of thing. So, let's say for instance...I'm just giving you an example...that I see a spirit, you perceive the spirit, you draw the spirit, as I'm bringing in the information about the spirit, you see? Or, you draw the spirit that you're perceiving, and give the information about the spirit to the individual. It's a beautiful art, and there's not many people that can do it. There was Carol Koroluk, I think her name was. She was famous in England and traveled all over the world with it. Next question, please? Does that help?"

Mike: "Yes, definitely. Um...well I guess I was hoping that a couple of more people would come through like my mom or dad, or my friends Dick and Marilyn."

Claudette: "Okay, first of all your mom and dad. Who would have worn a cowboy hat, please? ('Ah, my dad.') Your dad, okay. Was he a tall, slender kind of individual? ('Well, he wasn't slender, but he was tall, yeah pretty big.') In his youth he was. ('Yeah, when he was in his youth...yes, he was.') In his youth he was quite the macho guy. ('Yes, definitely.') So of course, he's going to come as a macho guy. (Claudette laughing) When you said mom and dad, immediately I saw this gentleman, and he's wearing a cowboy hat. So, that's his signature. ('Okay.') So, he comes in...and he comes in with...I want to say the *John Wayne* type of walk." (Laughing)

"Yes, and mom would have been shorter than him, but fairly tall...I would say 5'7", 5'8"...*yes. thank you*...but it's the father that is standing there and he's got his one hand in a pocket, and he's kind of standing there looking...'and so what are you going to do now?' kind of thing, you know? ('Yes.') But, I feel that your dad would have been a very rigorous person. Would have worked really hard. ('Yes.')"

"Who would have been in Saskatchewan, or the prairies? ('It could have been my in-laws.') I want to say, I'm seeing Alberta, please?...borderline Alberta, Saskatchewan.

('Hmmm.') I want to say, Alberta, and then I see Saskatchewan there. ('It might have been my father in law. I'm not sure') Okay, and then I have the prairies. ('None of my family is from the prairies.') But would have lived there, do you understand, please? Who would have been around Regina, Saskatchewan? Do you have a brother, please? ('I had a friend that lived in Regina.') Was he like a brother to you? ('Well, we were good friends.') He's in spirit now? ('I don't know. I haven't seen him in years.')"

"Alright...alright, father is standing there waiting to talk to me, kind of thing, and then peeking around dad, your mom is peeking saying 'I'm here too.' (Both laughing) Okay. Mom did a lot of knitting, or crocheting? ('Ahhh..') I'm seeing something in her hand that she is working, you know like knitting or something like that. ('She might have done a little bit of that...when I was young...') It would have to be grandmother.

('Yes, it's probably my grandmother.') Grandmother, because this is some body...I'm just seeing hands, I'm not seeing who's doing it. I saw mom peeking, so they're over there, they're not as close..the grandmother's the closest... she's showing me. ('Yes, grandma.')

Okay...arthritic hands...and she says 'it was good for my hands, to keep them busy all the time'. Okay. That's grandmother."

"And then father says, 'you know, I always wanted to achieve more than I did.', do you understand that, please? ('Yes.') And he says ' don't let anything stop you... don't let the fear...don't let...'. Because I feel with him he says 'no, that would be too risky because I have family, I have...you know'. So, he always played it safe, and he regretted doing that, because if he had taken the risk, he would have done better, do you understand, please? ('Yes.') And, so he comes with this regret, that he wasn't able to be everything that he wanted to be, and his advice to you is that 'don't stop yourself...keep going'. ('Yes.') Because you're very much like your father, very much so. ('Yes.') And there's a great love coming from your father, even though you may have had some disagreements, there's a very profound love for you. ('Yeah.')"

"Was there three in the family, please? ('Three, and then a very late one many years later...we had another one.') Okay, but the initial three...dad had one later in life... ('Yes. Dad and mom had one like sixteen years later.') Right, because I'm looking at the three. ('Yes, we were the main...') The main crew. (Laughing) That he kind of, I heard 'dictate to'... (Laughing)... not dictate, but basically took charge of. ('Yes, he wasn't around much for the later years.') It's like he...in his mind there's the three, and then the other one...because I felt like he passed...he can't have passed if he had another child, right?...he was not in charge of the that last one. So, it was a surprise for him just as much as his wife...being pregnant... or your mother... ('Yes.') Okay...and so...was there a girl, please?... in the three ...three boys... ('One girl, two boys, of the three...')...and so the last one was a boy? ('The last one was a boy.') So, boy, girl, boy was it? ('Boy, girl, boy, yes.) So, and it's like the three musketeers...like one after the other?.. ('Yes, two years apart.') Yeah, okay. What I have from your father is the pride of his three children. Unfortunately, he doesn't have that with the youngest one, right? ('Yes.') The three of you, there's a lot of pride...there's a lot ...because he was there to rear you...to be 'good citizens', quote, unquote...and to be the father, whereas the other one was there, and he didn't have anything against the child but it just wasn't to be. ('No.')"

"And then there was mom, who again suffered a great deal in her life. ('Oh, yes. A lot of...') A lot of pain. ('...lot of physical hardship.') Yeah, and, difficulty with back...my back is hurting, and so on...I hear also, 'I'm having trouble breathing with her...a lot of pain...but she says 'look at me now'...*yes, thank you*...and I feel that mom and dad would have danced... ('Yeah, yeah.')...they were dancers...they would have danced together...there was such a strong love between them. Ah... it was dad that went first, please? ('Yes.') Yes...there was a great like, emptiness with mom when he passed.

('Yes, definitely.) And, she never recovered from that...and it just never...the taste for life was never the same. So, she took charge of her life, making sure she looked after her family, but she says 'it was never the same'. So, in a way she was happy to go. ('Yes, she definitely was, I talked to her just before she passed.') Yeah, and she was ready. She was happy, and says 'I'm going to see him again', so ...*yes, thank you...* and she's showing me that she had the visual, she saw her husband. What was your dad's name? ('Bernie.') So, she saw Bernie, and that was like 'come on, honey'... you know, and he was there to greet her. ('Yeah.') There was just this excitement about seeing him, and just left. It's like 'I left peaceably'. So, though she suffered on the earth, she left peaceably, and she's very happy where she is. ('Oh, good.')"

"And so dad is saying that he is also been working to help as a healer. That he has been greeting...particularly one's that go quickly. ('Oh, yeah.') Did dad go quickly, please? ('He did, yes.') So, he wants...because it was such a shock for him. ('No, it was like three months, and then...he was good right up until the last week, and then...') Yeah. Did he...yeah...he was very perturbed about going, 'why is this happening, this shouldn't be happening'...like it was a puzzle...'how could this be, it's not meant to be', kind of thing. And so he still had that when he crossed over, and he got a lot of help from his own siblings, his own family on the other side, but he says 'I want to help others that cross quickly, either through... ah...you know....... ('drug addiction, or something?') not so much that but... either through war...that they're here one moment, then gone the next through... ('accidents?') yeah, quickly...or earthquakes, tsunamis...here one moment, gone the next. ('Right.') So, people that go quickly...he says, ' I want to be one of the greeters, to help them." ('Oh, that's good.')

"So, he helps them that way. He says we have the opportunity to grow on the other side. And, he says 'I want to help, I want to be...', and he was always one to be giving a helping hand, do you understand, please? ('Yes.') He was a generous person, he wasn't ...how do you say...he couldn't easily be fooled. He wasn't a fool, but he was a helper. He knew when somebody deserved a helping hand. And, he would always try, no matter how little he had,...he would always try to help. And, that's what he tried to instill on his children...to give a helping hand, when it's needed, but don't be a fool, at the same time. ('Yeah.') So, he comes with a great deal... and he says you have something of his. You have a book of his? I feel that he was an avid ...he loved reading."

Mike: "Yes. I think I do have a book of his. I think it was to do with the army, or something like that...or the war."

Claudette: "Okay, he says you have one of his books, and he says to look on page...it looks to me like page sixteen. ('Alright.') If it's not sixteen, reverse the numbers...so sixteen, sixty-one, because sometimes it doesn't come through... ('I'll have to look through my...I've got a lot of books.') Well, you take after your dad, you see, you love reading. ('Yes, I do.') And there it is, you write your own books now. It's all about getting on with it, and no more delays. Next question before we run out of time."

Mike: "The only other people I was hoping might come through was Dick and Marilyn. They were good friends of mine."

Claudette: "Who was the gambler, please? Who loved gambling? I'm seeing roulette. I'm seeing Las Vegas, that kind of thing. ('Ah...') Do you have a brother in spirit, please? ('No.') Somebody that was your friend, like a brother? ('I'm trying to think. Well, Dick and I were close. He went down to Vegas a few times.') Okay, but he wasn't addicted to it. ('No, he wasn't addicted to it.') But he would like to play...because I'm seeing Las Vegas. Did you ever go down to Las Vegas with him? ('No. I've got family in Las Vegas. Um...Oh, you know what? I wonder if it's my brother in law.') Okay. ('I just thought of it.') He would have loved gambling, or going to...not that he was addicted, but he loved the casinos. ('I think so, yeah.') I'm definitely seeing the sign LAS VEGAS. This is so clear, I can't get rid of it. It's Las Vegas. This is a man that would have gone to Las Vegas, or would have enjoyed going to Las Vegas, you know on one of those trips. ('This is one of those things that will come to me two days from now, but...') Let me see...can you give me more info." (Pause)

"Did he get married in Las Vegas? Do you know somebody that got married in Las Vegas? ('I can't think of anybody.') Okay. Do you have a cousin, please, that would have lived in the area, or would have got married in Las Vegas? I heard, 'I got married in Las Vegas.' (Pause). Okay, let me just get the information. Leave it with you, and … ('Yeah.') I have this gentleman. I'm seeing Las Vegas, I'm seeing... oh I'm seeing cars from the sixties, seventies, you know. I'm seeing one of those Ford...fifty-six kind of thing, like my brother had... ('Oh, yeah.')...but, it doesn't mean it was then, do you understand, please? ('Yes.') This is a man who would have liked the classic cars, the old cars as well. And, I hear that he either lived near Vegas, or he enjoyed going to Vegas. What is it, please? (Pause) Lived near Vegas. ('My brother in law.') Lived near Vegas, would have married near Vegas, or in

Vegas. He says 'No, I was married in Vegas.' Okay, so I want you...when you said brother in law, it didn't resonate." ('Yeah. Because he wasn't married in Vegas.')

"No, I feel that this is more of a friendship tie, or a cousin, it's a little removed. It's somebody that um...okay...and also loved Elvis Presley, drove you crazy about Elvis

Presley, because he was okay, but you know wasn't your thing. (Laughing). So, he liked to mimic Elvis Presley, do you understand, please? And, Elvis Presley was in Vegas. ('Yeah.") I feel that he would have wanted to go to the concert... would have went to the concert, not wanted, but went to the concert. It was Elvis Presley, and he had this thing 'hey, let's go to Vegas.' So, again, it's removed, so friendship tie. I feel that it would have been a friend to the family, friendship tie... ah...William...Bill. Anyways, I'm going to leave that with you, and his whole point is ' while you're here, don't take yourself so seriously, enjoy life'. So, he had this ability to enjoy life. He may have been a little bit excessive in certain things. (Laughing) But, he says ' at least I had fun '. ('Yeah.') He comes with that, and I feel very strong friendship ties, and again, I can't get rid of this Vegas thing. So, there's a connection to Vegas with this man. ('Yeah.') Either he worked there for his company for a period of time...or...may have met... *okay, thank you*... I feel that he worked in that environment for a period of time for a company. He was very much involved. It's big with him. That's his signature, this whole Vegas trip thing. And again, I married in Vegas. ('Okay.') Again, I get Bill...William...friendship tie. His message to you is 'live life, you never know how long you have.' Because as much as I say your here for the long term, still you get doorways, you can still make the decision. This is what I perceive, and this can change with time, alright?"

('Okay.')

"Now, with your friend Marilyn, did she have cancer, please? ('Yes.') *Yes, thank you*. I'm having a lot of trouble breathing, and so, and she says ' I'm fine'. ('Oh, good.') She had a sense of humor, please? ('Yes, definitely.') And, who would be Peter, associated with Marilyn, please? Is there a Peter? ('Um...I don't know'.) Okay. ('Her husband was Dick'.) No. Peter. She says there were a lot of jokes made about Dick.

(Both laughing) No, I feel...did she have a child, please, a boy? ('She's got a boy, yes. His name's Rich.") Okay, so Peter's not first, middle or last name? (' I don't know his middle name'.) It's definitely not the first, because you would know that. ('Yes'.) Peter...Peter what... I hear her say 'say hi to Peter'. ('Okay'.) Okay, I'll leave that on the shelf until she proves...because she's the one who needs to bring the two of you together, so you can say that she's okay."

"Also, that she made it across. This is a woman that didn't want to die. She fought this all the way, but it won in the end, right? ('Yeah'.) This woman was a vibrant woman, and was really perturbed about having the cancer, again this shouldn't have been. And so, she fought, and fought, and fought until she lost the battle. She went before her husband? ('Her husband went just before her. They both went pretty... within...very close to each other'.) She says that she was more advanced than he was. ('Yes. Nobody was expecting him to go, actually'.) Yeah, yeah. ('It was a shock'.) She says ' well we've been bantering about as to who went first and second'.

(Both laughing) He didn't want her to win. (Still laughing). ' I'm going to go, and you stay ', kind of thing, that bantering about. ('Yeah.') He had to win... he had to have his way, he had to be the one, kind of thing. (Claudette laughing) They're still arguing about this on the other side, right? ' You couldn't wait, could you. You had to make me go through this.' Instead of the other way around. So, he wasn't going to go through losing her, he was going to go first. ('That makes total sense, yeah.') So, she was very upset...angry with him going before her. (Both laughing) Because she had to deal with the loss, see? ('Yes, definitely') All of the papers, sort of thing. ('For sure.')"

"But, she wants you to know that they are okay, and that Dick is doing the best he can. (Claudette laughing) She says he's still in...what's the word...*say it again, please*...rehabilitation. ('Oh, okay.') (Claudette laughing, and whispering 'he still doesn't get it.') So she gets it a little faster than him. So he's still bucking the system right, so she's helping him on the journey. So, they're really full of...she's excited... she's the stronger of the two, and able to speak for the two of them. ('Okay.') Very, very...she wants you to know that she's excited to be able to communicate with you, and says 'tell everybody that I'm fine, that we're good.'"

Mike: "Because I stay...they actually have a place down in Birch Bay, and I stay in their place quite often, and I just want to say thank you for letting me use it."

Claudette: "Oh, well, again...there's a lot of respect...you know there was always this strong belief that you would never betray them, do you understand, please? That you were one of those true friends. ('Oh, yeah.') There's not many around... you know these true friends, and it's like kindred spirits. ('Right.') You were just one of those people that was...it was just a done deal...a knowing...and gratitude. There's also, she says, a book on the shelf in that place that you stay, that you are going to pick up, she says read it. I see the book, it's a hard cover, and I see it laying flat this way, instead of standing up. It's on the shelf, grab it, and read it, she says, 'it will help inspire you'...('Okay.')...and bring ideas, etc."

"I also feel please that...um...I know that John is your son. Would you know if you have another child that never drew breath? A little girl. ('I don't, no. That would be awesome, but...') Well, I have a little girl that's been...and she calls you 'daddy'. ('Really?') Yeah."

Mike: "I mean when I was younger I... ('Messed about.' Claudette laughing) Yes. So, it's possible. But you know, I never knew about it but..."

Claudette: "Yeah, yeah. What I'm receiving here is that it's a child...that never drew breath. That it was aborted, or miscarried, do you understand? And, it's a little girl. ('Oh.') And so, she's been coming to visit with you. She says 'you're now ready to find out that I exist'. ('Okay.') And so, she wants to be named, again. But, she comes to visit you like in the middle of the night...2:30, 2:25, 2:35...around that time period. Do you ever wake up around that time period? ('Yeah. Yeah I do.') And, I feel that it's her saying 'Hi dad, how you doing?' And again, she's a joy guide. She's very feminine...and she's very much the bouncy one...would like to...would walk beside you, hold your hand, and skip at the same time. So...and have a nice little pretty dress, be skipping, and have a little basket of flowers, or whatever...you know that old fashioned kind of look. So, I want to go way back in time, because she comes in with that old fashioned kind of skipping rope, not skipping rope... ('Can you see her? Is she blonde, er ...?') Yes, I see her. I see her hair as a light brown, close to...I would say about the same color as that wall unit. ('Okay.') And, I see her back...*turn around, please*...as she turns around, I see her with blue eyes, very sharp blue eyes. And, she comes and she has that...that smile that's kind of crooked, you know crooked smile...and then she says 'look at my nose, it's your nose'. (Both laugh) She has your nose, and she's wearing a yellow print, with flowers... ('Ahhh.')...and it's tied with a bow in the back. (' I almost pictured when you were talking about it...a minute ago.') Yeah. She's presenting herself with a beautiful yellow print, and there's a belt, you know from the dress, the one that ties in the back, and she has little white socks, with little white shoes. ('Ohhh.') But, she has a basket with wild flowers, not garden flowers, but wild... it's like the two of you walking in the field, and she's picking flowers, and putting them in the basket. ('Oh.') But, she says ' I come, and whisper to you...*daddy, daddy.* ' and then she kisses you on the side...yeah."

"So, she comes very lovingly, and she says 'now I want you to know that I exist, so give me a name.' ('Oh, I will yeah.') So, you have a meditation, call her forth, and then you can ask her, 'who's your mom?'. ('Yeah.') You ask her, and I feel that it's when you were more late teens, early twenties. ('Yeah, yeah. I can see that.') So, you know that you were... (Pause) ('Wild.')...feeling your oats. (Laughing) ('Yes.') And so, I feel that you wouldn't have known about the pregnancy. ('I didn't. I wouldn't have known about it.') And, I feel that it all had to do with an overnight thing. ('Hm.') That sort of thing, but I cannot get for certainty, whether it was aborted or miscarried, right? But anyways, I will leave her with you. Now, any other questions before we close?"

Mike: "No, I don't think so. That's pretty much all I had. We went over my...angels and spirit guides coming through to help me, and you sort of went through all that I should be doing an everything, so...and I do my meditations every day, and..."

Claudette: "Do you do your *GAPP* every day? ('Which'.) Your *GAPP*. Did I ever give you the *GAPP*?('I think you did mention the GAPP, but I can't remember now what it is.') It's *G* for Grounding... ('Oh, yeah.')...*A* for Ascension...*P* for Protection...*P* for Prayer of Intent. ('Okay.') G.A.P.P. So, let's do a *GAPP* right now, okay?"

"So, breathe. Take a breath. Ahhhh. Now, I want you to express that *Soul* essence which is love. Now say 'I am Love', and feel that love inside of your heart, and I want to see a *poof* of love come out of your heart. So again, 'I am Love'. Can you feel it in your heart? Just feel that little girl of yours near you. Feel John beside you. Feel your parents, feel your grandparents. Feel the love that they are sending you. Can you feel it in your heart? Yeah. Now, I want you to express this. I want you to say the words out loud, 'I am Love.' Let's say it together. (Both) 'I am Love.' So, it's not a statement, it's expression. What you are, a feeling, an emotion. So, say it again. (Both) 'I am Love.' Feel, *poof, poof, poof,* coming out of your heart. I can feel that *ahhh* happening inside of you. Stay with that, and know that you are surrounded by all of your family who are sending you this love, but I also have Angels around you, particularly, Archangel Michael by your right side. So again, (Both) 'I am Love.' So, the whole thing is to feel love before we do the *GAPP."*

"And as we feel this love, we want to extend it all the way down to the core of the Earth. So, I extend this love from my heart. *Feel* it go down through my body, through the soles of my feet to the core of the Earth. *Feel* it go down. Feel the gratitude, feel the gratitude in your heart to the 'four sacred elements'...so in your mind, from your heart, with the love vibration, you would express gratitude. "Thank you Mother Earth, Spirit of Fire, Air and Water, for nurturing my physical body'. And again, feel that love response come back to you. *Allow* it to come in. Ahhh. Did you feel it come back to you? Good. So now, just bathe in that. Allow it to go into your heart, and it just makes it that much bigger and stronger."

"And now, let's share that love some more, and extend that love to the core of Source. The Divine Source, whatever created you, the Spirit, the Soul, the Higher Self. In this case, we will command it with the love ' I ascend, ascend, ascend... 'I stand within the loving mind of Source...to the core of the Divine Source... not looking at it, but inside of that loving Light. In gratitude, and once again, we express with love ' Thank you Infinite Spirit, Divine Father, Mother, God, whatever you call that Source, for the nurturing of my soul, my spirit, my light.' And once again, feel the response of love come back to you. (Pause) Good. And now while you are within the loving mind of Source, ask for protection. And so, you would say, 'Infinite Spirit, Divine Father, Mother God, I ask for a Golden Sphere of Protected Energy be around me, so that any negative thoughts, psychic attacks, distant harm, bounce off, transform into positive, and goes back wherever it came from'. And then, feel yourself being enveloped in this Golden Sphere of Protected Energy." (Pause)

"Yes. And while you are there, let us ask, put forth your Prayer of Intent. What is it that you want and why? So, an example would be, ' Infinite Spirit, Divine Father,

Mother God, help me to lift up to higher ground, so that I may see the bigger picture, the reality of all that there is, so that I can make more concise decisions for the highest good of all'. It's just an example. So you may ask whatever is the assistance that you need in your life at this time...whatever you desire to fulfill, accomplish. But, you always want to say why. Another example may be, ' Infinite Spirit, help me to evolve, to see the reality, to break through the illusions, so that I may attain the greatest good for all.' (Pause) So, take a moment to put forth your 'Prayer of Intent'. (Pause) Good. And then, we always close with 'thank you for the many blessings that I have received and continue to receive with each breath that I take.'"

"Then you bring yourself back. It takes a minute, unless you get very verbal. It takes longer for me to explain it. ('Yeah.') So, I ask my students to do it first thing in the morning, and then you won't forget, because if you don't do it right away, you'll forget, you get busy with life and you forget. When you do it first thing in the morning, you set your day up, because now you are receiving love from both ends...the Earth and the Heavens, that feed both aspects of you...you the soul, and you the physical, which makes for a better day. So, even though you have the challenges, you deal with them better. The other thing with the *Sphere of Protection* is it enervates the interference from others...jealousy, etc., but it doesn't exempt you from your own karma. In other words, if you put out poop, you're going to get poop...if you put out good, you get good. ('Right'.) So, it helps you... at least you've got a fair chance to evolve and be on your journey. Now, I never gave you the piece of paper on that...I never gave you anything on that? ('Ah...I don't recollect that but...') Okay, I'll give you one. I give it to anybody who will listen to me... (Laughing)...and I'll leave that with you a say ' God bless '. ('Yes. Thank you.') So it's basically what we just did...('Uh hum.')...and again, it's not complicated...it's just understanding what you're doing. Try to feel the love in your heart, because love begets love. You radiate it."

Mike: "I'm never sure if...I mean I love, you know my family and friends, and everything else, and I know I'm getting tons of love sent my way and that, but I never know if I'm opening up to love..."

Claudette: "So, when we did this, did you feel that love in your heart...('I did'.)... did you feel that warmth? ('I had to really concentrate to...) Right. Because there is that, how do I say... ('It's almost like a barrier...) numbness, numbness...('Yeah, yeah')... because of the continuous pain. So, what we want to do, when doing this every day to open up, you think of something that would trigger it. ('Right'.) So, a child, or your dog, or your family...something that will help you, because some days it's harder than others. ('Yeah'.) Or, you'll think of some crazy little thing, right? Once you get that love going, and you send it out, and get it back from both ends, it becomes easier through time. Something will happen...you'll see a child smile, or an adult smile about something comical, and that will trigger it. Or you'll go to a movie, and you know how you can cry at movies...but you'll feel the same thing with that love thing, right? ('Right'.) That's what we need to do...because it's that vibration, it has to radiate out of you. So, I'll leave that with you, and say 'God bless'. ('Thank you'.)

It had been just over three years since I last visited Claudette, and I was ready for another session.

It's always exciting beforehand wondering who may come through and what new events may be in the future. When speaking of future events, they don't always adhere to a strict time frame. Again, we have free will and we are making choices every day. Some may be important choices...ie. jobs, marriages, and then there will be lots of smaller choices, like which route to take to get somewhere, or whether to buy something or not. Life transforms according to what choices we have made.

When we chose to incarnate on the planet, we had a goal in mind. We can reach that goal, but there are many paths that can get us there, all according to what choices we make along the way. There can be fast paths, or slower ones with many detours. We'll still get there, but it may just take longer. So when a future event is predicted, it's all predicated on those choices we make. It could be right on the mark, if all those choices worked out, or it could take a little longer with some round about detours.

Alright, now some comments on this last session.

That's hysterical that my grandmother is there again right off the back. It's like she's saying ' hey, I'm first. ' Also, my dog ' Buster ' again.

Another mention of going to England, which is definitely on my to do list. My mother was after me for years to get over there.

Also, the relationship angle. Claudette is right about me being pretty blasé about getting married again. I hope I can open myself up more when the right person shows up, and I'll recognize them.

My financial situation is much better with me working and now collecting my CPP (Canada Pension Plan) and OAP (Old Age Pension). I've got myself out of debt, with just normal monthly bills.

Love hearing from my son John. He says 'I'm a hard nut to crack', but it's not always so easy here. There's always some sort of contrast coming and going. With so much that I've been learning, I just deal with it a lot better than I used to. I try to keep a positive attitude, and instead of worrying over something, I just give it over to the Angels, and let them deal with it. If it's meant to be then let it be. And I find with that outlook things tend to run more smoothly with less aggravation. As I've gotten older, I've found that it doesn't matter to me what other people think. There are always going to be people that have different opinions, and that is fine.

As I've stated before, sometimes the other side uses pictures, so John coming through with the horse (mustang) was kind of funny. With my financial situation looking up, I decided it was time to get a car again. A few months before, I was in a used car lot, and saw a red used Mustang convertible, and for a moment considered buying it, before finally changing my mind and getting a 2007 Ford Escape.

I need to be more cognizant and on the lookout for messages that may be coming my way through other means. I really do feel more and more that I'm getting in touch with my spiritual self. I dream every night, and I am getting better at remembering what those dreams are. It's very easy to forget what you were dreaming if you don't make a concerted effort to remember. I know I should be writing them down. I've got to get in the habit of doing that.

I also know that many of my dreams involve those who have already passed. It's said that when we are sleeping, we astral travel, and that this shows up as a dream. I've had some pretty vivid dreams with family and friends.

It was when I was younger that I read a few books on the subject of Astral Traveling, and tried it for a long time with no success. Then I had that experience which I mentioned in an earlier session when I felt myself pulling out of my body and got scared and pulled back in. I do believe we Astral project, though most of us don't realize it because it's happening while we sleep. I look forward to having that opportunity again sometime.

There's the bit about the book, which is interesting in that this, and some other things were mentioned in past sessions (ie. Trip to England.) And, remember it's been three years since my last session, so for some of these things to come up again gives validation to them. Claudette can't possibly remember what was said in a session three or more years ago with me, when she's doing any number of readings every year. What's also interesting is that she originally saw me writing the book before I ever considered such a thing. Was it that original mentioning of the book that got me moving in that direction? Would I have ever written a book about anything if I had not gone to see Claudette? Food for thought.

I would definitely like to visit the *Arthur Findlay College* in England. The spirit art sounds very intriguing. I do love to paint now, and have been missing it lately having put it on the back burner, spending a lot more time on the writing. I actually look forward to the time when this book is finished and I can concentrate back to my artwork. It's one of those hobbies where you get started on it, and suddenly a few hours have gone by, and you can't believe it.

Once again it's nice to hear from my father, and his words of advice, and I am very much like him, though I'm sure I wouldn't have been as strict on my own kids if I had had any in the physical. As hard as he was with us growing up, he was a lot different once we reached adulthood, and it was always good to visit with him.

The only connection I have with the prairies is with my in-laws who have all passed. And I wouldn't have been surprised if they were trying to come through because I had a great relationship with them. They always introduced me as their other son. They were good people.

Claudette was right on when mentioning my brothers and sister, and the involvement with us, and then much less with my younger brother because of dad leaving and ultimately the separation. I think what led to their separation, was their financial situation, which wasn't good and put more strain on their marriage which was also having some other problems.

In better days, my parents did love to dance, and certainly enjoyed having a party.

And, in later years, my mother would talk to me from time to time about my father, and how she missed him. I visited with her just a couple of days before her passing, and she told me she had seen him in the corner of her room. She was tired of living and really wanted to go. She went peaceably in her sleep, and you can't ask for more than that. It's nice to think my father was there to greet her. He had passed about seventeen years before her.

My father was a big man and there was always a weight concern, but he did like to eat. So he was happy when he started losing weight, but then it didn't slow down. He went to the doctor's and was eventually diagnosed with cancer in his gall bladder. When they opened him up to remove it, the cancer had spread throughout his body. They sewed him back up and gave him the bad news. Anyway, he was given three months, and it was almost exactly that. Hazel, my father's common law wife, gave me a call around three, one morning saying dad wasn't doing very well. They lived in Sidney on Vancouver Island. This was late November and there was a lot of new snow on the ground. So while I was getting ready, Verine walked to an ATM close by to get some money for me for the ferry ride. It was a hairy ride out to the ferry, but fortunately there wasn't much traffic at that time of the morning. I got to their place a few hours later. My father had wanted to stay at home, and was actually pretty good right up to that last week. He had a care worker drop by every day for his medications. I went into his room, and it was heartbreaking to see someone who had always been a big man, just shrunken away to almost nothing. I'm glad he knew it was me, but he was very weak, so I made it a short visit to his room. I stayed with Hazel for a few hours, and then said I had to get back with the car, but that I would return. When I was in the ferry lineup to come home, I had the strongest premonition that I should turn around, but I didn't, and again, around three in the morning, I got a call from Hazel saying he had passed. I'm glad I got to see him before he went, but I'm sorry I didn't turn around when I got that feeling, so I could have been there for Hazel. Dad was seventy-six, and had always been healthy. I don't remember ever seeing him in a hospital, other than visiting my mother when she was having problems. I will have to look for that book that he mentions.

I was always amazed at how knowledgeable my father was. He didn't have a lot of schooling. He was the youngest in his family, and was pulled out of school at fourteen, where he would become an apprentice in the printing business. That's just the way it worked in England at that time with their class system. But he did love to read, and he obviously kept up with current affairs, because he could talk on just about anything that was going on at the time. He fought in World War II from 1939 until he was demobbed in 1946. I was born in 1947. With the situation in Britain after the War, dad decided to move to the U.S. where he had a relative who could get him a job in the printing business. Dad went first and when he was situated, my mother and I came over by boat several months later. I learned to walk on the boat, moving from deckchair to deckchair. A sister and a brother were born in New York, and we eventually moved to Ottawa, Canada when I was seven. Mom's brother had also emigrated after the War, to Canada.

Okay. The Vegas reference had me completely stymied. I could not think of anyone that loved to gamble and had got married in Vegas. Once again, it was quite awhile after this session when I was listening to it again, when I heard Claudette mention the name William or Bill, and there was a friendship tie, that it dawned on me that I had a friend in my teens named Bill. I just hadn't been thinking that far back. I had moved out West, but I had heard that this friend of mine had gone on to work for one of the Canadian broadcasting companies, and had done very well for himself, eventually directing and producing several shows on television. I had also heard that he liked to party, where alcohol , drugs and girls were part of the scene. I'm pretty sure I remember being told that he had been married more than once. It would not surprise me if this wasn't the person Claudette had coming through, because he had passed, I believe in his fifties through illness. This would be someone who definitely enjoyed life, and we all loved Elvis, and I have a good feeling that it would be him. This is something I may have to inquire about at some other time, if I can get in touch with some of my old friends. I wish this had have occurred to me at the time, for I would have loved to have communicated more with him.

I was really pleased to hear from Marilyn. She and her husband Dick were two of my very closest friends. They also had a place down in Birch Bay, along with our other good friends Glenn and his wife Donna. Marilyn, Donna and Verine all grew up together going back as far as early grade school. So, when we were all down together at Birch Bay, typically the guys would go golfing, and the ladies would go shopping in Bellingham. Then we would get together afterwards for happy hour and a fire.

Now Dick was a real card, and would constantly be doing little things that would embarrass Marilyn, especially if she thought he was having a few more drinks than he should. So, there was this banter back and forth, but there was never a doubt that they had a deep love for each other. Then Marilyn became very ill with cancer. It's funny to think they are still arguing about why Dick went before her, leaving her to deal with that.

It was a surprise when he suddenly went, and I can only think that he didn't want to be here without her.

Verine has the place at Birch Bay, and I was staying at Dick and Marilyn's place, kind of looking after the place when they were ill. Plus it gave me a chance to go to a place I really love. Since, they've passed their son Rich let's me continue to use it, which is much appreciated. There are always things that need doing, and I'm more than happy to take care of it.

I think the book she mentions is a book on birds which I paint on cards, usually for my friends Glenn and Donna on their birthdays.

Alright, once again I'm going to have Claudette bring me something that is totally surprising and emotional. Another child that didn't draw breath...a little girl. When Claudette describes her, I can really picture this little girl...not her face necessarily but the dress, shoes, hair and basket with wildflowers. Not long after this session I gave her the name Kaitlin Alexia, and I planted a bunch of wildflowers in a big planter down at Birch Bay. It's her garden. I don't know who her mother would have been. What can I say, it was the sixties. I call her Katie, and now I've got two kids that call me dad, and are Joy Guides for me. Wonderful.

I've mentioned the GAPP in a number of previous sessions, so it was good to have Claudette go through it completely with me. What I trigger it with, is a couple of dog commercials I've seen on TV that always have me laughing or smiling. So, this gets me in the proper mood, and I usually do it first thing upon awakening, and it's very fast. Like Claudette says, it takes longer explaining it than actually doing it.

Once again, very happy with everything that went on...who came through, and this wonderful feeling that this child revealed herself to me. I know one day that she, John and I can go walking through a field of flowers together, with probably Buster and Toby running ahead.

FINAL SESSION WITH CLAUDETTE

It's Monday, July 06, 2015, and this will be the last session with Claudette as far as this book goes. Claudette has now moved to Penticton, a small city in the southern interior of British Columbia. So, we will be doing this session by Skype. When I asked Claudette about how this would work with us being so separated, she replied that there was no problem, spirit isn't concerned with distance. I also know that there are a number of spiritual teachers and different mediums that do their sessions this way, and from much farther distances.

It's 1:00 o'clock, our agreed upon time. I've got my recorder set up, and I am starting the Skype now.

Claudette: " There we go." ('Can you see me all right?') I can see you good. Can you hear me? ('Yes, fine.') Good. Good. So, we're in the process of finishing our move here. Things are still in their boxes. ('So, you've just moved to Penticton?') No, it's my second move. I had moved in September, renting a condo, but the lady sold her condo, so I had to move again." ('Oh.')

"So, Mike we know how this all works, right? (' Yes, for sure.') Okay. So, we're going to do a few breaths here, to just detach from this physical world, and move into a sacred space where I can get the Higher Guidance, and nothing from this physical world will interfere with what we're doing. Okay? ('Okay.') So, we'll breathe in the Loving Light, and we'll exhale any tension, anxiety, stress, whatever may be going on. (Both inhaling and exhaling with the 'ahhhhh' sound). Good. Breathe in the Loving Light...and release. That's it. Breathe in...and release the stress, anxiety, etc. etc. That's it, all the poo,poo...and one more, two more breaths, *I hear*. Breathe in. (Both breathing in, and exhaling with the 'ahhhh' sound) Good,again, breathe in... good. And now, we're going to do three breaths, with the intent of detaching from the physical world, so that we can move into a beautiful altered state of awareness. Again, and to merge and blend our frequencies. So, I breathe in the Loving Light, and I exhale with intent of detaching from the physical world, so we can have this pow wow without any interference. So, again we breathe in and detach, detach, detach. Again, breathe in...detach, detach, detach...we'll deal with all that stuff later. Again, breathe in...good."

"And then I'll go into my prayer of intent, and we'll begin. So, expand into the alpha state of awareness, I ask my Higher Guidance to step in to our beautiful Golden Sphere of Energy. (Pause). Infinite Spirit, Divine Father, Mother God, we ask for a blessing on this sitting. We ask for the highest and the best clarity of mind, direction, and understanding, amen." (Pause)

"Mike, if I may begin...as I was saying the prayer, I got this release of the negative energy around you...I just feel like the energy...the healing energies came in and just said...*'let that one go, let that one go'*. Would you understand that, please? ('Yes.') I just feel that there's been a lot of tension, a lot of *'errr'* kind of stuff around you, and I just feel that that energy came in, and there was a release...ahhh, of peace...a little bit of peace coming in. I also had a...I want to say a Spirit guide coming in. I don't feel that it is a loved one, but a Spirit guide coming in, and I feel Mike that you have come to a point where that communication with your Spirit guide is becoming stronger. Would you understand that, please? ('Yes. Actually, right now I'm tingling all over.') Yes. I just feel that your guide is a Higher Guidance here that is wishing to work through you, with you for the greatest good of humanity, etc. type of thing. And I feel that...there's a...did you ever get this feeling, this need to journal, please?"

Mike: "You know, I know I should be doing that more. You've told me that in the past, and ah...I mean I have been writing a book, but I haven't been journaling, you know on a daily basis sort of thing."

Claudette: " The reason why I ask that is because of the book, because I feel that you are supposed to be writing a book, and you just mentioned that you are writing a book, or have been writing a book. And, I just feel that there is more material coming through, but with your Higher Guidance. So, I feel that the material that you have written will shift into this...um material I should say or wisdom...*yes, thank you*...knowledge and wisdom that will come from a Higher Guidance. Would you understand that, please?"

Mike: " Yes, and that is one of the reasons I wanted to get in touch with you, is about this book, really."

Claudette: "Okay. So, go ahead and ask the question about the book then please."

Mike: "Well, I'm just wondering if this book is going to have any relevance for anybody other than myself maybe, and a few family members, that's all."

Claudette: "Right. I feel that the book that you have written was the initiation, if you like...a view, the training...you know the dedication to writing, the healing process as well etc., and yes it will be beneficial to your family, yourself, but it's a healing journey for you. Would you understand that please? ('Okay.') However, having been a healing journey for you, what we need to do right here, is to publish it nevertheless, and just self publish...it's so easy to do it now, right? ('Right.') And that it will draw the people that need to read this experience, need to read this material. I feel that what's exciting is that it has triggered that authorship of yourself. It has triggered that need to write some more. ('Okay.') Yes. And, I feel that as you do this, you will publish at least a minimum of three if not ten books. Do you understand? ('Wow.') So, I see like a library of shelves, and I see this one book that is...how you say...the book that you have written right now is your special initiation...it's your prize. ('Okay.') So that will be in its own case...a memory, or what have you. But, as you have done that, and healed from it, what I see happening, is this energy coming from this book, and creating these other books, what I mean by that is, it's not going to be the same material, or the same information, but more information, expanded information...a greater expansion of awareness, and wisdom. Would you understand that, please? ('Okay, yeah.') And, I'm excited because by next year at this time, you will have written that one book...that first book. And I feel as you publish it, and as you bring it to various book places where you are signing the book and all this... I see you doing lectures...I actually see you Mike doing lectures in front of large groups, expressing, and coming from your heart...and also, I see the light coming in within you to channel. Have I not said this to you before?"

Mike: "Umm...a little bit...yes, you have. ('Yeah, it's still...') But, I need to get with somebody you know to develop some of these things."

Claudette: "Right. Well...well, I'm going to be offering a once a month workshop in Vancouver...so attend. But, I feel that the other thing about public speaking. ..you see the thing about you, is that your very sensitive. ('Right.') So, through the crapola that has happened in your past life...in the past...not past life...in the past, what it has done is made you shy...not wanting to make a fool of yourself, not wanting to look... ('ridiculous.')...odd. ('Yeah, right.') Yeah, so what we want to do is take you know that...that course from...what is it called...public speaking thing...('Dale Carnegie, is that one of them?')...something like, not that one...but the other one...('I know what you mean.')...you know what I mean, right?...just participate in that, to help you break through this. Because that is your destiny... that is well, destiny...quote, unquote...that's your journey, to be able to speak to large groups etc., and though that may not seem possible at this time, it is there."

"And remember that what I am perceiving is what you've already created."

"So, what you have done is initiated, opened up the channels to light. Now you have to open up the *throat chakra* to express. And so...but remember when you're doing your lectures, and demos, and workshops, because you're also going to be doing workshops. You're going to be channeling your Higher Guidance at the same time. So, what you want to know in your heart, is that it's not all Mike; it is a team effort from your Higher Guidance that is standing there with you, and also that *soul* Mike that's merging with the *physical* Mike, and so past is past, let's move forward...you know, get over yourself, and let's move forward. Do you understand, please?"

('Yes.').

"What I also feel...are you presently in a relationship, please? ('No.') No...I just see a relationship coming in. And it's like you've got your arms like this...

(in front warding)...I want to, but I'm afraid to. (Me laughing) ('You've mentioned that before actually.') Okay, well there you go. It hasn't changed, it's there, because I don't remember a thing that I have said to you. ('No, no, I realize that.')"

"What it's saying is 'open your mind, open yourself to infinite possibilities'. Eliminate the restrictions. Eliminate the conditions. Eliminate the constraints. And so, 'you know what, as I radiate love and light, I will draw to me love and light'. ' I'm also a wiser man today. I know the signs, I know that what I don't want is to be co-dependent upon, or rely on somebody else. I want a true partner, who will stand strong and confident, and yet share, and be a partner'. That's what you need. Somebody that will support, somebody that you will support, but not be co-dependent. Do you understand, please? ('Yes.') And, usually emotional traumas of the past, you had relationship, or there was co-dependency. But, what I'm seeing is it's not there in your future Mike, so, allow yourself to say...' Okay I trust, I trust that I have the ability to draw to me the right relationship.'"

"And, what's so exquisite about this is that you form a great partnership where you can spend the time in that meditative or alpha state of awareness to receive the information, and your partner is going to help you to, you know write it or... how can I say...to watch over you while you're doing that." ('Okay.')

"So, it's not today, it's not tomorrow, but it's on its way. And, I get a six with that, and that tells me it's six days, six weeks, or six months, and I want to go with the six month period. ('Okay.') Because you're still apprehensive. You need to let go of your guards before you actually welcome the relationship. ('Right.') If you have to look at somebody and say 'well is that the person, or isn't it', it's not. You will feel it in your chest. You will feel that 'woooo...' type thing. But don't jump into the bed with it, do you understand? (Both laughing)"

Mike: (Still laughing) "That's been a problem when I was younger, for sure."

Claudette: "No wonder it's been said 'don't jump in there'. Just allow that friendship to develop. Allow it. And, I want you to look at life as an exploration, not as an uhhhh horrible destiny type thing. And look at every day 'I'm exploring this journey...I'm exploring this life...I need to explore, I need to explore love, I need to explore light. I need to explore my psychic abilities, my mediumistic abilities '."

"I want you again, and I'm sure I've said this to you before, to embrace your sensitivity as an asset. ('Yes.') It's not a curse. However, do your *GAPP*. Have you been doing your *GAPP*?"

Mike: " I have actually been doing it, yes."

Claudette: " It helps, doesn't it? ('Yes, yes.') It just creates the day better, and it helps to deal with the ups and downs of life. But remember that the ups and downs of life I just said, are not negative, we make them negative. ('Right.') So, what it is, it's an exploration to help us evolve. And so, as we evolve, we are able to help others do the same, alright?" ('Yes.')

" Now, I also have...*yes, thank you*...I have a grandmother type vibration there with you, please. Do you have a grandmother in spirit? "

Mike: (Me chuckling)"Yes. She's usually always the first one to come through."

Claudette: (Laughing) "Yeah, yeah, as I looked at you, I saw this grandmother, 'when are you going to tell him I'm here' kind of thing. So again, she comes with a great deal of love, and just has so much confidence in you, and just knows that you are heading for the best time of your life. Do you understand that please? ('Okay.') And, the only reason that won't happen...wouldn't...not won't, but wouldn't happen is your doubt. Because you have...it's all free will. And you have the ability to change things, or flavor things with your thoughts and actions. Yes? ('Yes.') Okay. But then grandmother comes and she's kushing you on the side, and she just loves you, she just loves you. She embraces you." (Me chuckling)

"Then, next to her, there's a gentleman who's tall, slender, and I feel more of a fatherly type vibration, so, I feel grandfather or father. ('Probably father.') Yeah, somebody that would have been very structured...very structured. This is the way it is...da, da, da, da. There's no yes or no, this is the way it is, you know? ('Yes.') Take it or leave it. This is the way. (Claudette laughing) Very structured. But again, it didn't mean that he was less of a person, it's just that's how he was brought up, and that's how it had to be. ('Yes.') And he did not understand the variations. Very tunnel vision here. But, I feel that this gentleman though, he may have been a challenge...um had a good heart. ('Yes.') Yes. And would be a good provider.

Would express...less frequent than most people...but would have...sometimes the words would have been in a cutting edge, you know what I'm saying?"

('Mm, mm.')

"So, he comes and he says ' I now understand.' Does that make sense to you, please? ('Yes.') He says those words, 'I now understand. Forgive me for not knowing, or understanding in the past, but know in your heart that I do understand now, and that my love has just grown even greater for you.'"

" I hear, 'I am proud of you, and I am investing all of my energy towards you, to help you move forward to your greater success.' Do you understand...('Oh, good. Yes.')...please?" ('Yes.')

"So, do know that the family is there, and I do see that beautiful rainbow over your head, and to me in the rainbow is written '*Success*'. And now it just explodes into beautiful, colorful...um...like we just had on Canada Day...what is that called?... ('Fireworks.')...fireworks, thank you, beautiful fireworks...and for me that translates into success, but also celebration, ' here I am, I made it through.' And it doesn't mean that life just ends here, but it continues, but it helps me to have that strength and courage to go forward."

" There will be sad days, there will be good days, but there's that strength within you. All the poopie stuff in your heart, you've taken out. Do you understand, please? ('Mm, mm.') I just feel like cleaning out the cauldron, cleaning out all that crap at the bottom. But you see that that would indicate that your frequency has elevated. You see? ('Okay.') As your energy shifts, that crapola can't stay there. So, having done the steps to heal yourself, to be a better channel, to be a, you know a great ambassador of love and light, what you've done is...um...erase...not erase, because erase means you never...you know...we don't, how can I say, erase the past, we look at it...it is history, but it has no effect on us. And that's what you've done, is you have healed, transformed some... a lot...a lot...I would say seventy per cent of that emotional crapola. There's a little bit left, and that's about trusting and allowing. You see? ('Right.') And know in your heart that this is there to be."

"Have you ever thought of adopting, please? Adopting a child?"

Mike: " Ah...not really, no. I'm getting a little old for that I think."

Claudette: "Well, how old are you now, if I may ask? ('Sixty-eight.') Ohhh, bless your soul. (Both laughing) You're not that old. Okay, sixty-eight...seventy-one is your next change. So, from seventy to seventy-one. It has nothing to do with the age, or hitting the seventy type thing. But I want you to know that...did you just turn sixty-eight, please? ('Yes, a few of months ago.') Okay, as you moved into your sixty-eighth, what has happened is that you have reached the half way mark. So, the adjustment from sixty-five to sixty-eight, is a new vibration, etc... as you hit the mid mark, it's an *ahhhhhh*...it's like a relief. I got the worst over, do you understand? ('Yes.') Because sixty-five to seventy-one, as I told you before, is all about change, shifting, moving, you know that kind of thing. So be aware."

"Have you ever owned an apartment in New York city? ('No. No.') Are you aware of anyone that lives in New York city, please? ('Mmm, no.') No. I can see you in New York city. The reason I ask these questions..."

Mike: "I lived there when I was a little boy."

Claudette: "...Oh, okay. I see you in an apartment in New York city. Not to say that you're going to move there on a permanent basis, no, so I feel that there's going to be a lot of transactions, or business work, or what have you, to do with New York city, okay? ('Okay.') And so, I feel that there's at some point, there's an investment in an apartment in New York city. ('Wow.') Bless you. That means your quite wealthy by then. (Both laughing) (Me. 'No kidding.' Both still laughing) I think it's just as bad as Vancouver. (House prices) ('Yeah, wow, yeah that is something.') But, I do feel that your home base will be Canada. And, I do see you staying in the West, but I feel that you will also have an apartment in the East, and I get New York city. I can't see how far ahead that is, but immediately got New York city, an apartment, but you're not on your own there either. So you're already into your relationship."

"And so...um...there's been a lot of controversy with you, would you understand that, please? (Hesitant, 'Yes.') Yes, and I want to say that you want to take the best, and leave the rest. So, not to just live in this controversy. Let it go. You do your part, and let it go. ('Okay.') As you do that, you say 'okay I've done my part, I surrender it, let it go and move forward.'"

"I also feel that there's going to be on your journey a lot of legal documents. These are contracts, basically. And I feel that they are contracts associated with your work, with establishing yourself, etc., etc."

"Are you retired from your normal quote, unquote 'work'? ('I am, yes.')

Yeah, and I feel that retirement has served you well, do you understand that, please? ('Yes.') Again, I would ask you please, to release any negative thoughts you have about your physical self, or your handsomeness, whatever. (Both laughing) Erase, erase, erase... okay, get rid of THAT one alright? And start linking in more and more with the heart felt vibration. ('Okay.') What will bring your success, Mike, is the heart felt vibration, remember that, okay? Because the intellect is great, but it must marry the emotional body, so to be a formidable team. Remember we live in a duality world, a world of duality, okay, and so that there will always be the other side of the coin. For us to stay on the light side of the coin, we have to come from the heart vibration. So now, let's get to your questions before we run out of time."

Mike: "Ah...one of my questions...well we went on with the book...but one of my questions was, I was really hoping maybe that both of my kids who were never born, John, and last time I talked with you, a little girl came through, and she wanted a name, so I gave her a name, I call her Katie, but...so I was just wondering if John and Katie were available...or there?"

Claudette: "When you mentioned them, your children...you mentioned Katie, my heart went...*whooooo*...and I feel that Katie has really attached herself to you, you understand? So, when you asked that, there was this embrace, not that the boy isn't, it's just that Katie felt so special when you gave her the name, do you understand, please? ('Okay.') So she feels...daddy's girl kind of thing. ('Oh yeah, good.') So, she's really excited about that...and John is kind of looking at her as if to say 'come on, get over yourself', that kind of thing." (Laughing)

Mike: "So those two know...they know that they're...?"

Claudette: "For sure. Absolutely. There's no secret in the Cosmic world. There's absolutely no secret. They definitely have met, and there are times that they come together, and you'll feel one on one side, and the other one on the other side, and there's also a dog, please. (Me laughing) Do you have a dog in spirit? ('Yes.')

Okay, so I've got the dog in the middle, I've got the two children, I got the girl and the boy. So, John and Katie...John isn't it?

('Yes. John')...John and Katie and the dog. The dog's name is? ('It's either Buster or Toby, there were a couple of dogs.') It's Buster. ('Buster's the one that usually comes through I think.') Yeah, this is Buster. (Claudette laughing) Toby was the other one? ('Yeah.') Yeah, so I heard in the background *'I'm too busy, I'm too busy.'* (Both laughing) ('That would be him.') Yeah, he was a charmer. (Both still laughing) ('For sure.') Buster was more the close, the loyal friend type thing... ('Yeah, exactly.')...the other one is *'I'm busy, I'm busy.'*"

"But I also feel that as you work, you know the lectures, and the work I said about your books, etc., when you're actually doing the lectures, your children and your dog will be standing there with you. ('Oh, good.') And the wonderful part is you'll feel that...you'll feel it, isn't that wonderful that you'll be able to actually say ' Ah, my family is with me.'"

Mike: "Yes. I mean I picture the three of us like walking in a field or something together. ('Yeah.') I mean I'm not sure exactly what they look like, but I can picture us together, you know."

Claudette: "Absolutely. So, it's like your *spiritual garden,* if you like. And they love nature as much as you do, and of course, they are going to assist in every way possible for you to be happy.

The other part, is that your partner that is on its way to you, will understand all of this. This is not going to be strange. You have to have a partner who is open, it doesn't mean they have to do the work, but that they are open and supportive. And this is what I alluded to earlier, is that your partner is going to watch over you as you go into this trance, or altered state, doing the channeling etc.

But, I feel with you that the books that are coming up, are going to be a deeper trance state, if you like. So, I just feel you going deeper, so that the information is clear and...ah...clear...what's the word I'm looking for...pure, if you like."

Mike: "So this would be like the *'Abraham'* ...?"

Claudette: " Similar, similar. I feel that it is wisdom like that, you know whether it's *Lazarus,*or *Abraham,* or many of the wonderful teachers that have come forth. Yes, it's that kind of thing. It will start with the combination of both of you, and then it moves into a deeper state of trance. So the first book is a combination, the second book is deeper, deeper, deeper...it just gets deeper. And I feel that your Higher Guidance will identify themselves, and what I like too though, is that you will have evidence...where you will actually have a visual of what this Higher Guidance is. Because for you, it's important to have a visual, do you understand, please? ('Yeah, yeah.') And so, your Higher Guidance is an energy field, right? So, what your Higher Guidance will do, is take on a form to assist you in that relationship."

(Here, we lose contact with each other, when Claudette gets another call coming in. A few minutes later, we are reconnected.)

Claudette: "Hi Mike, sorry. ('No problem.') You went on hold, because someone else tried to reach me on Skype. (' Oh.' Chuckling) I never had this experience."

Mike: "Yes, I'm not real familiar with using it myself. I use it with my grand-daughter occasionally."

Claudette: "Okay, last thing we said?"

Mike: "Um...we were going about the channeling...('Right, right.')...and the Higher Presence."

Claudette: "Do you have any questions about that?"

Mike: "Ah...no. I have a question...I'm just wondering...like Katie...I don't know who Katie's mom was. I don't know...you told me last time when I was meditating to...ah...try and have her come through with a name, but...I'm not very good at that...(Chuckling)...I didn't get a name coming through."

Claudette: "Okay, with Katie...um...okay, were you in a relationship...?"

Mike: "When you told me last time, it was like one of those one night stand things."

Claudette: "Okay...I get eighteen. Do you remember that age group? ('Yeah, yeah.') And, I feel that it's more...I got the age eighteen...('Okay.')...around that time. Do you recall having...?('I do, yes, yes.')...*Okay, yes, thank you.* I just got confirmation. Did you have a visual of a woman in your mind, please? ('I did, yes.') Okay, when you had that happen, I got confirmation. ('Okay.') I got *'yes'* that's who it is." ('Okay. Wow, yeah, okay.')

Mike: "And, I'm just wondering also...John...I knew his mother...but I'm just wondering, how she has been, or can he tell me...does he keep in contact with her like...does he look over her...?"

Claudette: "No... I feel that his mother has passed. Are you aware...have you...? ('No. I haven't seen her in forty some years.') The sense I get with his mom, is that she is in spirit. ('Oh. Okay.') That's the sense I get from John...that she has passed, and is carrying on her soul progression in the spirit world, and that his focus is on you. ('Okay.') That he has asked to work with you, because he didn't have an opportunity to do it on the physical level."

"Now, the other thing is that I was going to say earlier, is that your children will take on the form that you would be impressed upon. ('Okay, yes.') So, remember that the spirit is an energy field...it could be an energy sphere...it could be...you know they don't really have a form, however they will present themselves in the form, based on what their genetics would have been. ('Right, I understand.') So that your visual of what you feel they look like, is what it will be."

"These two children have this exquisite love for you, because these two children are so innocent, you see? They have that true knowing of love. They know the real you, not the physical you who has been through the challenges, the trials and tribulations and so on, and that has had the scars and what have you. They know the soul you, they know your real power...they know, and they want to help you bring that soul power out, do you understand, please? ('Yes, okay.') It just feels so exquisitely beautiful. Can you feel it as I'm saying it? ('Yes, yes I can, yes.') Excellent. Yeah, yeah."

"Now you meditate on a regular basis? ('I do, every day, yes.') Right.

That's what the kids were telling me...John and Katie were telling me that you regularly meditate and they sit with you. ('Oh, good.') Okay. And the dog like... owwwwwwwww...(Both laughing)...he wants to join in the fun. So remember that when you sit in meditation from now on, you have two sitting, plus the dog. ('Okay.') Then, you have your Higher Guidance around you."

('Right.')

"Now, for whatever ails you physically, you need to ask your...before you go to sleep, ask the Divine Source, as you say your Prayer of Intent, to send you the expertise, the Healing Doctors to come and heal you while your sleeping. ('Okay.') Do you understand that, please? ('Yes.') I feel that you feel uncomfortable with your body, that the... ('Yeah, I...')...the aches and pains..."

Mike: "...Yeah, I tore my rotator cuff about six months ago, and it really bothers me at night. It's not too bad during the day, but at night it really gets me."

Claudette: "Okay. So that's where you want to...as you lay down in your comfortable position, ask for *the Healing Doctors* to come and work on...you have to ask for them to do it, okay? ('Okay.') Ask them to come and do the healing, and you ask the highest expert, the one that is most knowledgeable in whatever troubles you. And, just do that every night, so that *the Healing Doctors* come, because they will. All they're waiting for is your request. ('Okay, good.') Which will help you, and even though the pain may go away for a while, just keep doing it anyways, because you want to get to the root of it."('Right, right.')

"Remember that any shoulder issue is survival. ('Hmm.') So, shoulder is your *root*, is part of the *root chakra* , if you like. Anything to do with ankles, wrists, of course the hips, where the *root chakra* is, shoulders, it's all *root* related. So it's survival, it's you know, on this earth plane and whatever."

"And basically what you have been doing in the last six months is healing the *root chakra,* dealing with survival issues. ('Okay.') Which is all based on scars, and previous life experiences, etc., okay?

('Yeah, that's interesting.') It needs to be done for you to open up and trust again. Remember earlier we said seventy per cent...that's great. That's really good. So you've been doing your homework; you've been working at it and it's showing."

Mike: "Yeah, I've got to the point where I know the past is the past...I mean that's not who I am now, that's who I was...and... ('Excellent.')...it's gone. You know, I've gotta live for right now and..."

Claudette: 'Exactly, it's in the moment, and being in the moment, you have past, present, and potential future, right? ('Right.') There's no separation, it's all there, it's now, and every breath, every thought creates your future. So what we've been talking about is your potential future. And it's so strong. That means that you're determined to create...to fulfill your divine plan or your divine mission. And that is to write the book, to lecture to...you've got an energy that people love. People love you. You say ' oh, what's wrong with them, do I look funny or something?' No, you just have that energy, right? ('Hm, mm.') Do you notice how people gravitate to you? To the point where you just want to push them away." (Claudette laughing)

"But you have that energy field that will assist you in being successful. So, you allow it to even radiate that much more, but at the same time you have your *Golden Sphere* around you...your *GAPP*. So as you have that, it just eliminates the negative thoughts from jealous people or people that you know like la, la, la, la, thing, right? ('Right.') So that it transforms and goes back in a positive. Remember that any situations in your life, you must have that win, win situation. Whatever challenge that you may have, you say 'okay, what is the win, win situation here?' That is the way of the *Light Worker*. Okay, so we need to have a win, win situation all the time, and remember that you are offering information, you are not dictating, right? ('Right.') You offer, let it go, offer let it go."

"At the same time as you write your book, what you're doing is showing them how. So you're showing them how to fish, instead of giving them the fish. So, what happens is when you're doing your divine plan, to help people elevate themselves, to move into their higher selves. Next question, please?"

Mike: " Well, I'm just wondering...I don't have any exact questions. I'm just wondering if there are any other people around, family or friends, or anybody that want to come through, and..."

Claudette: "I know that your son's name is John, but do you also have a friendship by the name of John, or Jonathan. I've got a gentleman coming forward. I feel that he would have been a smoker in his younger years...slender, I had a chest condition, I'm having trouble breathing, so it's either lungs, or heart...I just feel it's...(Gasping)...having trouble breathing. ('John, John. I'm trying to think now...') If it's not John, or Jonathan, it's the letter J. for sure. Oh, and I want to... *yes, thank you*...twenty-four, twenty-five...you were...when you were twenty-four, twenty-five...I'm asking is it you or him that were twenty-four, twenty-five, around that time period."

Mike: (Chuckling) "Those were hazy years...in the sixties...um, John."

Claudette: " If it's not John, it's the letter J., and I feel it would have been a work environment...okay, I feel a work environment, I'm more of a laborer, rather than an administrator."

Mike: "Oh, I did know a John, yeah. John S."

Claudette: "Oh, good. I just got a hit. ('So, he's passed, then?') Yeah, that's what I get here. So, I'm asking John why he is here, and he says 'I want to thank you, Mike for understanding and helping me out.' ('Okay.') This is a gentleman that would have had some troubles in his life... ('Yes.')...a challenging life. And, he comes in gratitude to say 'thank you for being there for me, and for actually helping me out when nobody else would have.'

(Hesitant 'okay.') Your kindness, your generosity...he says 'I so wanted you to know how much I appreciated all that you did for me, and I just had to come and tell you this.' And he says that 'anytime just call on me, and I'll be there for you.' (' Oh, wonderful, yeah.') So, I feel that he would have passed with a chest condition. I can't make out whether it's lung or heart...*yes, thank you*...I just get cancer with him."

Mike: "Okay, Yeah, I haven't heard anything about him in a number of years so...I didn't realize..."

Claudette: "Yeah. So there is this gentleman, and I hear there is this aunt or auntie of yours coming forward, and I feel that this aunt would have had a sense of humor.

Do you have an aunt in spirit, please? ('Yes. I think I've got two or three of them.') Alright. So this aunt, again...Jesse, Margaret? ('Not Nan...not auntie Nan?') Okay, she had a great sense of humor, please? ('I believe so, yes.') And she would have loved hats? I see her wearing a hat, and she just thinks it's the best thing going. (' Did I know her really well, because...?') I hear that 'there were a few encounters.'"

Mike: "Okay, because there was an auntie Phil that I met. And...um, then auntie Nan, I was a little more closer to. I'm not sure if she's passed yet. The last I heard, she was still alive.'"

Claudette: "Let me just get some more information here. This auntie...I see a farm background, please. I see like a country...country background. (Yeah, there's a couple of aunts that I had, that I didn't know at all.') Do you know Saskatchewan...does Saskatchewan have anything to do with this? ('No. I don't know anybody in Saskatchewan.') Alright, let me just...I see the prairies, and then I see Manitoba. I see prairies...I feel there was a time where this aunt would have been in the prairies. I just feel that there wasn't that closeness between the two of you, but that you have crossed paths. And, the biggest thing about it...*yes, thank you*...definitely farming kind of background...I'm seeing a cow. I don't see a whole herd of cows, but I see one...(Claudette laughing)...that's following her everywhere. I'm getting the name Mag...Maggie. Okay, so I'm just going to give you the details, and maybe you can check. And I'm asking 'well why are you coming?' She says 'because this ...*what do you call*...this, well I'll say young man, but she has her own word for this, and I can't grab it. It's like 'this young man needs a greater sense of humor.' ('Oh.' Laughing) Because there is a lot of similarities between the two of you, and I can't get rid of the name Maggie. So Maggie comes...did your auntie Phil have a sister, please? ('Yes.') Do you know what her name was? ('No, I can't remember. It might have been Maggie, or Margaret.') So, Maggie would have been her nickname obviously. So check in with the Phil background there. I feel that she would have passed, you know fairly...before everyone else. I don't want to say early, because that would imply that she was young, but she passed before her sister. ('Yeah.') And hence again, the reason you might not have known her, because she was out in... ('She lived in England, as far as I know.') Ah, okay. So that would also...the prairies may be the reference for me, you know the country kind of thing. I can't get rid of it, it's there. So, I'll leave that with you. But, she comes...her message to you...and she comes with a great deal of love and a sense of humor...and she says 'use your humor, particularly when your stuck.'

(Laughing) 'Do not take yourself too seriously,' she says. 'Laugh at your'...she's got a word, but she's saying too fast... she talks fast...(' I was going to say foibles, laugh at your foibles.')...something of the kind, but she's saying it so fast...she's a fast speaker. ('Right.') I can't please them all. (Laughing) So, as you research her, just know that you have crossed paths somehow. ('Okay.') You do not recall, that you have crossed paths?"

" You need to go to England, I hear. ('Yes, I've been told that in every session, probably.) Oh, is that right, eh? There you go. ('I know I'm going to go one of these days. It's on my to do list, for sure.') Well, for sure. Put it in darker... darker, bolder letters... England. So, Maggie here wants you to go to England. You need to go, touch in with your roots, blah, blah, blah. Again, I see the plane flying from New York to England. (Oh, okay.') You may be in residence, you know six months there, six months here, or three months there, nine months here, who knows right? ('Yeah.') I don't see you becoming an American citizen. No, that's not what I'm saying. ('No. I don't see that.') But your work will take you to New York, more often than none.

So, the investment pays off. ('Okay.') It's like an investment, so that you have a place to stay, or family and friends, whatever... can use the apartment as well. ('Right.') Next question, please?"

Mike: "I don't have anymore questions, um. I did want to talk to you about, you know the book that I've been writing. ('Yes.') The book that I've been writing is about all of these different sessions, um that we've had together. This would be the fifth one, I guess. And, I've transcribed a lot of those, putting my own thoughts into it, but transcribing our sessions, and I want to know how you feel about me using your name in the book? Are you comfortable with that, or not?"

Claudette: "Yeah, I don't have a problem as long as it's not abused, you know what I'm saying?"

Mike: " No, it's...I've put in like 'Claudette', and I've put in the 'Wings of Dove', and what the 'Wings of Dove' stand for, and then basically it's you...it's a literal transcription, it's not me making up anything you've said or anything else."

Claudette: "I trust you with it, Mike. I hear...it's okay to go ahead with this, and to trust you with it, right?"

Mike: " Okay. I'll give you a copy, before I show anybody else, if you like?"

Claudette: "Oh, for sure. My only concern would have been, that it was put in a negative vein. ('No.') I truly love the work that I do, and I trust that *Spirit* would inspire you in the way that needs to be inspired...to do that. And so, yes by all means...ah, it helps for you to also say 'well this is not a thing that I created, it was also brought to me', or whatever the case may be."

Mike: " Yeah. It starts out basically, with a bit of a traumatic experience I went through...how I wound up getting your number...then our first session... and then, you know second session, third and fourth sessions, and some of my thoughts on the sessions, which are not negative at all. I mean... ('No, no.')...some things I didn't understand, or something, or whatever. ('Yeah.') But, basically that's it."

Claudette: "Your thoughts are **your** thoughts, right? And, it's just that any medium doesn't want to be marred by anything, right? ('No.') There's enough negative people out there that...('Especially in...there's a lot of charlatans out there...and that kind of thing.') Of course, of course."

Mike: "But, I thought I'd ask. I didn't...I could have put just 'C.'...capital C, and left it at that, and not used your name at all, but I thought I'd ask you and see how you felt about it."

Claudette: "You know I don't feel bad about it. I feel...I'm asking *Spirit,* and I hear *'go ahead'*. ('Okay.') So, I trust you, and you know, it's all Karma, right? ('Right. Oh, definitely.') So, I trust that the Universe is allowing this in a good vein."

"All the work that I do, I can only offer and let it go. That's the thing, and we hope for the best. We also know that everything can be shifted and changed, based on thoughts, actions, and whatever...fears. And, you know what...it's perception, we will perceive based on our vibration, our frequency, do you understand, please? ('Yes.') Whoever reads the book, will perceive based on their frequency, and we can't control that. And you know what I'm public. I can't hide in a corner. I'm out there sort of thing."

Mike: "Well, I'm putting myself out there, too in this book, And, ah…I know there will be people…I know there will be skeptics. I know there will be people that will say, 'well, that's kind of crazy', or whatever. But you can't please everybody…ah, that sort of thing."

Claudette: "That's right. It's like the two sides of the coin, Mike. There's always going to be the fanatic, there's also going to be the extremist. But, there's also people that are open minded. And, I believe that as you create this book, and you offer it with *Love and Light,* that the right people will read it. ('Good.') That's what we have to believe in. That's what you have to put out there, and say ' I offer this to all who are ready to read this book.' ('Right.') You know, and so it is."('Okay.')

Mike: "And the last thing is just about your development classes, I guess."

(Here Claudette gives me information on her upcoming classes, which I intend to attend starting in September. Claudette also gives me information on a retreat in 2016 which I would like to put in here because it's interesting as to what she does.)

Claudette: " Next year, I'm doing a retreat, and I believe June, 2016…I believe it's 10th, 11th, and 12th weekend. ('Okay.') I'm going to send a memo out to people…all my previous students, and what I'm asking is for people who are really interested in making that development. People that have invested that time, as you have with your meditations, and 'yes' I'm going to do this, you know, because the people that I want in the class…are not people that it's just 'oh, I just wanted to know what it's about'. It's people who are determined on improving their abilities, working with their abilities…see you would be writing, somebody else may be platform work, somebody else may be healing, or whatever."

"But, what are the basics? What are the foundations to help you be good at what you're doing? It doesn't matter what it is. What are the foundations…how can I move into a greater awareness of the *Unseen World,* whether it's *Higher Guidance, a Spirit person, or an animal*? But, mostly my objective is so that people can work with the *Higher Guidance.*('Okay.') And work, as in channeling or whatever… however way that they want to evolve."

"There are some people that are already doing public work, but they don't feel that their work is, you know strong enough. They want even stronger. And so, when they see me doing a demo they say 'well, what is it that you're doing, that makes you this way?' The bottom line, Mike, it's the 'heart felt' pleasure, love, that you're doing the work in. What I love most to do is teach. I love it. I love it. When I'm teaching, all my *Higher Guidance* are there to tell me what to say...to help me, because Claudette gets in the way, so 'well they're going to do this', and *bang*, it's changed because the *Higher Guidance* say 'No Claudette, no. That's the human perspective, let's move into the Higher perspective.' I would be excited to see you join the group in September. Anything else, Mike?"

Mike: "No, that's great. Thank you very much."

Claudette: "Let me just summarize here. So, as I close here, I want to say that you've got the forces with you. And you have to feel it in your heart, and not to be...how do I say...apprehensive about things. Do you understand? ('Yeah.') Look at it as an exploration, an adventure. And when you get that apprehensiveness... oh but, but, but...because everybody else tells you the contrary of what you're feeling...go with what you're feeling." ('Right.')

"Follow through with that. Do your *Protection,* your *GAPP,* and allow yourself, to experience, to explore. Instead of the word 'meditation', use the word 'exploration'. ('Okay, good.') And please focus on your pineal gland. ('Right.') Okay, so do your meditation, just...no, erase the word focus, sit with your pineal gland..."

Mike: "Yes, I get tremendous...um...that chakra, the brow chakra...it's always been dominant with me. I get a tingling there, like nothing flat. I mean it's..."

Claudette: 'So, what you want to do is acknowledge that, and just listen to your breath, and move into...I want to sit with my pineal gland, just like a feather sits on your hand...because if you focus, then you're not allowing. ('Okay.') Okay, so I've got to erase the word 'focus' here. So, I'll leave that with you, Mike, and happy trails, and have a good summer."

Mike: "Yes, same to you. Thanks."

It had been almost two years since I had seen Claudette. I've been working on this book, transcribing the sessions, and giving my thoughts about what has transpired. I decided to do one more session to add to the book. So here are my thoughts and feelings on what took place at this sitting.

It's very interesting to me that the first energy to come through is a Spirit Guide, and it has to do with writing a book. This was another reason that I wanted to have another session with Claudette was to speak with her about this book, and how she felt about it, because she is the biggest part of it, and whether or not she would be comfortable being mentioned in it. If I didn't have her permission, then I couldn't use her name, but just the letter 'C', and no mention of her ' Wings of Dove '.

Now the other thing with the book, is the importance it has had for me. By going through these sessions again, and writing my thoughts and feelings, it has opened me up to so much more spiritually. I know that I have had some amazing experiences, and I do feel that there are some latent sensitivities to the spirit realm. It's time for me to expand these senses.

I am blown away with the thought that there will be more books down the road. The part about lecturing is a little intimidating. And, Claudette is quite right about me not wanting to make a fool of myself, especially in front of a lot of people. I believe I would be alright talking to smaller groups. I may have to look into that Speaking course.

Since the last session I have been retired for about nine months. I am now sixty-eight, so don't know how long I would have been able to work anyway but not because of any health issues. The thing is that now being retired, I have the time to take Claudette's workshops and try to develop and expand my awareness.

Just to touch on *Higher Guidance/Higher Self...Higher Guidance* is that part of your consciousness that is in contact with *Spirit*, with Source Energy/the Universe/ God. If you believe in reincarnation, then all of our past lives are part of that *Higher Self*.

There's that relationship business again. I guess it's going to happen at some point, because it's been in every session. So, I've got to open myself up to this, and just let it be. Get out of my own way.

Oh Nanny. You know, I only knew her for a short time, but there must be a tremendous bond with me, because she is always right there, chomping at the bit to come through to me. As I've mentioned before, I was only five or six when she returned to England, but I do remember her, and wish I could have had her with us a lot longer.

And, of course my dad who has always been there also.

Before I start my daily meditations, I always ask to be surrounded with the *White Light,* and then I say, ' I release all negativity, all blockages, and all restrictions to the *White Light* that surrounds me. I release and let go of anything that does not serve me well '. So, this must be doing something, because Claudette sees me getting rid of a lot of as she says ' emotional crap '. Also, when I'm starting my meditation and feeling relaxed, I say, ' My body rests and refreshes itself, whenever I consciously relax. I am relaxed now.' This is acknowledging that the cells in my body are constantly rejuvenating, renewing themselves.

The apartment in New York is pretty exciting. Never would have pictured anything like that.

I am very happy to hear that John and Katie are together, and of course I can't forget Buster. That definitely would be Toby saying ' I'm too busy, I'm too busy '. As I've stated before, I can't hear him, but that sounds just like something he would say, if a dog could talk, which I now understand that they can communicate on the other side. He was absolutely the smartest dog I've come across. He had a box full of toys, and you could ask him to get different ones by name, and he would rummage through until he found them. And if I need a laugh or something to smile about, I just have to think of him and the empty mouthwash bottle. I don't remember how we ever gave him an empty mouthwash bottle, but whenever we wanted to watch the six o'clock news, he would grab that bottle and start crackling it with his teeth. It's like ' you're not paying attention to me, so I'm going to do this ', and it made a racket. As soon as you tried to grab it, he would take off down the hall to the other room. If you didn't chase him, he would be right back crackling it. So you'd have to chase him around the house until you where both tired. It was his game. He was one of a kind.

The channeling is very interesting. I can see myself at some point getting into something like that. Even more reason for me to start these workshops with Claudette. I need to get into an environment where I can see others with their talents and where there is more energy in the room to help me in my progression.

I now know who Katie's mom is. I remember exactly who that person was when I was eighteen, and again, as soon as I thought of her, Claudette got confirmation of that is who it was. I wish I had known about the pregnancy. I am sorry this person had to go through that. Another person I would apologize to if the moment ever presents itself. It's been fifty years. I am not sure why Katie chose this particular time to come through to me. Maybe the time was just right for her, especially now that I already had John coming through. Anyway, I'm thrilled to have them both. I was also sorry to hear that John's mother had passed. It's been a lot of years, and I truly hope she had a good life up until her passing. It's nice to know I have the two of them, and Buster with me when I'm meditating.

That's good to know about the *Healing Doctor* guides, and I am now asking for their help every night before I go to sleep. My shoulders are getting better but they're not back to normal, and it is taking longer than what the doctor called for, which may have to do with age, or more than likely dealing with those root chakra issues. Speaking of which, aside from this injury, and some occasional aches and pains, I feel good.

Okay. Another friend coming through. Sometimes I think I have more friends on the other side than I do here. It took me a few minutes to remember who it was, but when Claudette mentioned around twenty-four years of age, it came to me. As I said his name, Claudette confirmed it. John was another buddy, part of a group of guys who hung out together, and lived in a house with myself and two other fellows. At that time we all smoked. As we get older and get married, we tend to drift apart from some of our friends. I heard that John had moved back east, I believe around the Thunder Bay area. I also heard that he had got married, but that his wife became ill with cancer and passed. Once again, I have this friend thanking me for being there for him, when I don't really remember doing anything in particular. It's almost like on the other side, they just appreciate the least little thing. All of them are so thankful and willing to be there for you. It's a nice feeling.

Another session with the prairies or farm country being shown, and this aunt figure named Margaret or Maggie. I am going to have to try and find out if my dad had a sister with that name. I have or had relatives in England that I don't know at all. Another reason for me to head to England. One of these days. I mentioned in an earlier session that there was a Marge...a friend of my mother's who was sort of like an aunt figure, but she was from England, but there could have been farm country there. And again, the only family ties to Saskatchewan were my in laws, but not with a Marge connection.

The last part was just talking to Claudette about the book, and I was very happy to hear her comments and her agreeing that I could use her name. I will send her the transcript when I'm finished. Claudette is very passionate about her calling, and her love of teaching.

I have to start thinking of my meditations as explorations.

I was happy with this session as I have been with all of them. It has been an eye-opening experience, and there is much ahead in this journey. Claudette's classes are definitely important, if I want to start moving myself in the direction all these guides and family members have been stressing to me.

CLOSING THOUGHTS

What a distance I have come. From a place eleven years ago of dark despair, to a more knowledgeable and happy individual. With **The Universe** trying to get my attention without success, and placing me in a position of desperation, to saving me and getting me on the correct path. And that's the way I look at it now. So many steps along the way. All of those books, written on a variety of subjects, but all having relevance to me at the time. The circumstances that brought me to Claudette is remarkable in itself. Because of the passing of Verine's daughter, and Verine's doctor recommending two psychologists that might help her deal with her loss. To Verine picking one, who eventually happened to be the one to suggest Claudette, and so from there. I do not believe in coincidences.

I had some interest in the paranormal when I was younger, and then life got in the way, and I completely fell away from it. The time may not have been right, but when it was time for me to start fulfilling what I was meant to do, and I wasn't paying attention, I believe The Universe stepped in and said ' It's time. Now get on with it. ' Suddenly, I was in an uncomfortable situation with a bleak outlook at the time. It got me through that and started delivering to me all the tools I needed to get me back on my path. Yes, there was some procrastination, and some doubts, and it probably has taken longer than it should have, but I've got a much clearer picture now of who I am and what lies ahead.

This book is not going to be for everyone. I hope there are parts that you can take and use yourself, parts that may hold some meaning for you. That there is something here that may help you or confirm what you may have already suspected. If you find that this isn't resonating with you, hold on to it anyway. There may come a time, even years later where you can pull it from the shelf, dust it off, and find that part which holds some relevance.

There are always going to be skeptics. Hell, some of my own family and friends may be doubtful of what has gone on in these writings.

There is just way too much information for anyone to have made this sort of thing up. There isn't a doubt in my mind of those family members or friends that came through, that that's who they were, even including my pets. I could almost feel their personality coming through. Many of the sessions had some repetition from previous sessions, and Claudette couldn't possibly remember what had been said two or three years prior.

The transcripts are accurate. After that it is my own thoughts of what has transpired.

Another thing I would like to touch on is my belief in the importance of meditation. I think you will find that fifteen or twenty minutes a day of slowing your breathing and quieting the mind will make a big improvement in your overall well being. Doing that twice a day, even better. There are so many benefits to meditation from stress reduction to better health. More and more people are reaping the advantages of meditating. There's a wealth of information on the internet. The website *Mindfulness,* which I got from a recent *60 Minutes* episode, to *You Tube,* where you will find every kind of meditation imaginable. I think once you get yourself in the habit, you won't want to miss a sitting. Just the complete relaxation of the body is worth it alone, and it's when the body is completely relaxed that good things happen. The cells in our body are constantly rejuvenating; it's when that body is totally relaxed that the new cells really go to work.

I'd like to go through a healing meditation with you now. But I want to stress this is not to take the place of anything your doctor may be prescribing, if you are under a doctor's care. This is merely another tool to assist you.

Start out by sitting in a comfortable position. If you need to, you can lie down, but I've found that when lying down, it's easy to fall asleep. Now let's start by taking some long, slow breaths. Breathe in through your nose... (Pause)... Breathe out through your mouth. Breathe in... (Pause)...Breathe out. Do this a few times. Now, we want to start relaxing our body, starting at the top of your head...slowly feel your scalp relax, your cheeks, your face, your chin. Now your neck and shoulders, which can hold a lot of tension. Feel a comfortable warmth as you relax these areas. Feel them relax. Now feel your arms relax...your elbows, wrists and hands. Feel your body relax...your stomach...your hips. Feel your thighs, knees, shins, ankles, and feet relax. Your whole body is relaxing. You can feel yourself sinking into your chair or sofa. Continue with a natural slow breathing.

Now, I want you to picture yourself on a sandy, warm beach. You are alone. It's a beautiful day. There is a slight, warm breeze. You can hear the water lapping on the shore. You can hear the breeze ruffling the leaves. You lie down on the warm sand and look up to the sky, which is a beautiful blue, with a few wispy clouds. The warmth of the sand is penetrating through your body. You feel this warmth and know that this is a healing energy flowing through you from head to toe. This energy is healing wherever there is any illness, disease or injury. Continue to revel in this wonderful healing flow of energy. (This may last for several minutes). If your mind tends to wander, simply acknowledge that, let it go and go back to picturing and feeling. Once you are satisfied with the experience, slowly, counting back from 1 to 5, feel yourself coming back to awareness, feeling better than before.

At times, the mind just won't quieten down. Look to some of these thoughts, because they just may be *Guided Messages from the Other Side*. It just may be our Guides trying to get something through to us – some action to take, or the answer to a problem we may be facing. Is that voice in my head my own thoughts or a Higher Guidance? I have had days where no matter how much I try to quiet my mind, the thoughts just persist. Now, when that happens I start paying attention to what those thoughts are. In most cases it has had a bearing on something I'm dealing with. It has even added some context to this document. Don't dismiss it out of hand.

So, who am I now? I am still that person, who likes to do his art, likes to golf, likes to have a cigar once in a while, and have the odd drink. I do my ordinary day to day chores and live my life as much as most of us do. I am not a religious person, but I do believe in a Higher Source of Energy... the All That Is/God/the Universe. I guess I can call myself a spiritualist, because I believe in spirit. A definition of *Spiritualism* is: a system of belief based on supposed communication with the spirits of the dead, especially through mediums. This doesn't rule my life, but as Claudette told me, it is a merging with my physical self. I do my meditations everyday because I enjoy it, and feel I get a benefit from it, but I am also trying now to increase, enhance, improve my intuition, my sensitivity to spirit. I want that two way communication with my guides. I look forward to the coming years and what they hold for me.

Lastly, I hope there is something that you as the reader can take away from my experiences.

Blessings to all of you.

Mike.

ABOUT THE AUTHOR

Mike worked for over forty years in the stock brokerage business. He was vice president of trading for a local brokerage house, and served as a governor on the floor of the Vancouver Stock Exchange. He had some interest in spiritual matters in his younger years. Mike currently lives by himself in Vancouver.

Printed in the USA
CPSIA information can be obtained
at www.ICGtesting.com
LVHW050528170524
780507LV00039B/738